Church Divinity $\frac{1990}{1991}$

GRADUATE THEOLOGICAL FOUNDATION

BR
45
.C55
1990

The Church Divinity Monograph Series is sponsored annually by the Graduate Theological Foundation of Indiana.

The Graduate Theological Foundation is a tax-exempt religious research and educational institution approved by the Indiana Secretary of State from whom the Foundation holds incorporation.

All correspondence regarding the Series or related matters should be addressed to The Reverend John H. Morgan, Ph.D.(Htfd.), D.Sc.(London), President, Graduate Theological Foundation, Ancilla Domini, Post Office 5, Donaldson, IN 46513.

CHURCH DIVINITY 1990-91

Edited by

John H. Morgan

ISBN 1-55605-166-2

Printed in the United States of America

Typeset by M & M Typeset, 14041 C.R. 8, Middlebury, IN 46540.

RESPONDENTS FOR PAST ISSUES

Harry Adams, Associate Dean
Yale University Divinity School

Professor Robert T. Anderson
Michigan State University

Dr. Brigitte Berger
Wellesley College

Professor Robert F. Berkey
Mt. Holyoke College

Professor John P. Boyle
University of Iowa

James Carpenter, Sub-Dean
The General Theological Seminary

Professor John B. Cogg, Jr.
School of Theology (Clarmont)

Arnold B. Come, President
San Francisco Theological Seminary

Professor Richard Comstock
University of California at Santa Barbara

Professor John P. Crossley, Jr.
University of Southern California

Robert J. Daley, S.J.
Boston College

John Dillenberger, President
The Harford Seminary Foundation

Professor John F. Priest
Florida State University

Professor Wayne Proudfoot
Columbia University

Professor James E. Royster
Cleveland State University

Professor W. R. Schoedel
University of Illinois

Professor Nathan A. Scott
University of Virginia

Donald W. Shriver, President
Union Theological Seminary (NYC)

Professor Eugene A. TeSelle
Vanderbilt University Divinity School

Bard Thompson, Dean
Drew University Graduate School

Professor Gibson Winter
Princeton Theological Seminary

Professor Henry J. Young
Garrett-Evangelical Theological Seminary

EDITOR'S NOTE

It is with no little delight that I edit this tenth collection of essays by aspiring new scholars in the field of religious studies. This project, the CHURCH DIVINITY MONOGRAPH SERIES, has been developed specifically for the purpose of enhancing and encouraging theologically creative students who are still very much in the midst of "refining" their skills in theological expression. This Series, which is an annual event under the sponsorship of THE GRADUATE THEOLOGICAL FOUNDATION in collaboration with WYNDHAM HALL PRESS, is designed to provide a forum within which theologians, while still in their student years, might have an opportunity to compete for recognition and through early appearance in print gain the attention of the scholarly community.

The distinguished **RESPONDENTS FOR PAST ISSUES** have been selected not as specialists in the areas in which they have responded but rather because of their reputation of scholars and teachers in religious studies. For their kind willingness to participate in this Series, I am most appreciative.

This competition is open to any student enrolled in a fully accredited graduate theology/religion program of a seminary or university in North America. The competition announcements go out in the autumn of each year. The response continues to be encouraging. In the spring term of 1992, an announcement of the 1991-92 National Student Essay Competition in Divinity will be sent out again to all relevant institutions. All faculty persons are invited to encourage their students to compete.

HOLY CROSS DAY 1991   JHM✝

TABLE OF CONTENTS

THE STRUCTURE AND EVOLUTION OF CALVIN'S
DOCTRINE OF THE ATONEMENT:
Findings from Four Documents

Jonathan Tice
Western Theological Seminary

CHAPTER ONE

OUR ULTIMATE ADDICTION: A Study of Augustine's Notion of Concupiscence

Marty Miller Maddox
Andover Newton Theological School

ABSTRACT

In this essay I interpret Augustine's idea of *concupiscentia,* disorderly desire, as the inbred moral sickness which gives rise to all our enslaving habits. I depict concupiscence as the Addiction of addictions.

INTRODUCTION

Concupiscence is a key element in the theological anthropology of Augustine of Hippo (C.E. 354-430). No other Western thinker so greatly emphasizes *concupiscentia,* intense desire, as the distinctively Christian technical term for our human propensity toward actual sin.[1] Although he uses the word imprecisely during his writing career, Augustine generally uses concupiscence to refer to the Pauline lusts of the "flesh" versus the "Spirit."[2] For instance, in oft-quoted passages of his **Confessions,** Augustine portrays concupiscence as disorderly desire which militates against our spiritual longing for God.[3] In his writings against the Pelagians Augustine stresses concupiscence as an inbred moral sickness which can serve as both a consequence and a cause of sin.[4] Particularly in the sexual sphere, even in marriage, concupiscence plays a major role as a sign of the disintegration of human personality, a pointer to corrupt human nature inherited from that ancient sinner, Adam.[4]

This essay seeks to answer the question, "From a Christian perspective, does Augustine exaggerate the force and significance of concupiscence?"[6] My answer will be both "Yes" and "No." Yes, especially in his later writings, Augustine does overemphasize the working of concupiscence in the sexual sphere,[7] to the extent that he comes close to equating sex with the transmission of sin. But, no, Augustine is not wrong in describing concupiscence as a universally inherited human sickness,[8] an ailment which induces us to sinful preoccupation with the delights of this world's goods. My thesis is that in the notion of carnal concupiscence Augustine correctly identifies the theological root of all human addictions. As the expression of the soul's unhealthy attempt to invoke a harmony of the body and its appetites (via the "flesh"), concupiscence stands for the inbred Addiction, or anxious clinging to earthly goods, which gives seed to all kinds of compulsive behaviors.[9]

In the following I will describe Augustine's notion of concupiscence. Special attention will be given to Augustine's *On Marriage and Concupiscence* (C.E. 419-420, a two-book treatise which has exercised a great influence even apart from the Pelagian controversy. Such a work does not amount to a *locus classicus* of Augustine's view of concupiscence; but taken together with another anti-Pelagian writing by Augustine, *On Original Sin* (C.E. 418), it serves to illustrate Augustine's obsession with concupiscence as counter evidence to Pelagius' erroneous description of free will.[10] *On Marriage and Concupiscence* also represents the mature Augustine's insistence upon the force and significance of concupiscence in his "slogging match" with the upstart Julian of Eclanum.[11]

Next, I will evaluate Augustine's exaggerated role of concupiscence in reference to sex. While accepting this as a weakness in his account, I will go on, nonetheless, to offer a hypothesis of concupiscence per se as a properly Christian designation of our inherited human tendency toward compulsive behaviors. I shall note, finally, that all addictions are rooted in our most basic human Addiction: sinful concupiscence, i.e., willfully obeyed, inbred, disorderly desire which leads a person into habitual, corrupt, and often ruinous enjoyments of inferior goods serving as replacements for God.[12]

AUGUSTINE ON CONCUPISCENCE

From the classical Latin *concupiscere,* meaning to strive after, to aspire to, to covet, to long for or desire,[13] concupiscence, in its technical, strictly theological sense, is spontaneous desire which precedes a person's free decision and resists it.[14]   John J. Hugo distinguishes Augustine's peculiar notion of concupiscence:

> Concupiscence, therefore, in Augustine's thought, is the disorderly pursuit by the several appetites of their proper natural goods, a pursuit which, since the loss of integrity, is

difficult even for the grace-filled will to contain within the prescribed limits. This concupiscence, tending to exuberance and turbulence (one of Augustine's favorite words) leads readily to disorder, diverting the will from God. There are always the two elements: a turning to creatures that causes a turning from God. Concupiscence is not, therefore, as the Pelagians maintained, a merely natural vigor by which the faculties appropriately seek their own goods; it is a powerful vital energy that spontaneously rises to excess, tempting the will from God. The diversion from God constitutes its formal evil.[15]

We may gather the following from Hugo's statement: For Augustine, concupiscence is (1) an inner human moral problem which (2) persists even in the life of Christian believers and (3) leads to alienation from God. As an ongoing consequence of original sin (but not original sin itself) concupiscence is an inborn proclivity toward idolatry. As an enduring temptation to love created things apart from their Creator, concupiscence serves as a perverted love and a snare for *charitas,* the true love of God.[16]

Throughout his writing life Augustine attempts to describe the nature of empirical sin, the present inner moral problem of human nature, with various terms. Early on he chooses to define our state of sin as *libido* and *cupiditas,* passion and desire, and he later tries to make these two consistent with the less Plotinian and more Christian *superbia,* pride.[17] In disputation with the Manichees he begins to emphasize a triad of sins as a description of the root human fault: namely, the "triple concupiscence" of carnal lust, curiosity, and pride found in I John 2:16, corresponding to Plotinus' attributes of the soul's fall.[18] In the *Confessions,* for example, Augustine speaks of the lust for power, the lust of the eyes, and the lust of sensuality and he claims that "the chief kinds of iniquity. . .spring forth. . .from one of these, or two, or all three together."[19] As Augustine matures, however, he uses increasingly the word *concupiscentia* to denote the irreducible existential human dilemma of the lusts of the "flesh" versus the "Spirit" (cf. Galatians 5:17; Romans 7).[20] It is important to note that the later Augustine depicts the moral sickness of concupiscence as an inheritance from Adam and not an individual achievement.[21] The weight of concupiscence is, therefore, a burden transmitted to us at birth, and it continues with us until we die. We may diminish its influence by way of various ascetical disciplines, but we will never escape it this side of paradise. Even in our most hallowed institutions--e.g., marriage-- Augustine finds the debilitating influence of sin's dis-ease.

In the most complete patristic work on the married state, *The Good of Marriage* (C.E. 401),[22] Augustine staunchly defends the three great values of marriage: procreation, fidelity, and sacrament. In his opinion the goodness of marriage lies in its primary purpose to produce children, its praiseworthy law of mutual faithfulness, and its indissoluble bond between spouses, which prefigures the union of Christ and His Church.[23] He mentions that lustful, nonprocreative sexual intercourse within marriage is venial sin. As such, it is pardonable. Sex outside of marriage, however, is mortal sin.[24] But continence from all intercourse is the best way, according to Augustine. While adultery and fornication are illicit and unprotected by the three great marital values, which act as a safety net for fleshly weakness, marital intercourse, even for procreation, still lacks the merit of total continence, which allows one to enter into "a holy and pure association" with others.[25] By asserting celibacy as the highest life, Augustine hopes to refute the unorthodox monk Jovinian's teaching which puts marriage on a par with virginity. And by calling marriage at least a secondary good, Augustine hopes to avoid the charge that his own Christian teaching is Manichaean because it promotes an overly wary attitude toward concupiscence.

But as Augustine approaches what we would now call the age of retirement (age 65 or over), he is indicted again for his "Manichaeism."[26] This time his accuser is the brash bishop of Eclanum, Julian, "the last and most formidable of the Pelagian controversialists,"[27] a young man in what we would now call the prime of life (around age 35). Julian is upset with Augustine's insistence upon original sin's present reality, e.g., in a persistent, troublesome concupiscence which complicates our decisions of free will. Julian is especially disturbed by the first book of *On Marriage and Concupiscence*, which Augustine addresses to Count Valerius, "on learning that he had been informed of the Pelagians that they charge us with condemning marriage."[28] Julian writes four quick books to answer Augustine's work. With mere extracts of Julian's first response, Augustine crafts the second book of his treatise. Again, Julian wastes no time by publishing eight books in a rejoinder sent to the Pelagian bishop Florus.[29]

In Book I of *On Marriage and Concupiscence*, Augustine sets forth the evil of carnal concupiscence in contradistinction to the good of marriage.[30] Against "impudent men" (Pelagians) who impudently praise "shame-producing concupiscence" Augustine declares that marriage has an enduring existence independent of bodily desire.[31] He lifts up the gift of conjugal chastity in devotion to God as the excellent form of marriage, with the natural aim of marriage being the procreation of children.[32] He finds that the marriage of Christian believers "converts to the use of righteousness that carnal concupiscence by which 'the flesh lusteth against the Spirit'."[33] While fleshly lust is condemned within marriage, says Augustine, marriage itself remains a sacred institution, for concupiscence comes from sin (not from marriage).[34] In no way does concupiscence belittle the good of marriage. Like a lame man limping after a good thing, marriage is hampered by lust in its struggle to generate human offspring. But we do not label the man's gain of the object evil because of his unfortunate injury; nor must we name marriage as evil because of the weakness of concupiscence.[35]

But neither must we celebrate concupiscence in light of the goodness of marriage.[36] For concupiscence is often a disobedient, rebellious lust against the will's direction to do the good (e.g., procreation). Because of disorienting desire we cannot proceed straightway to fulfill God's purpose for marriage; instead, we must often wait for concupiscence to set our body in motion to willfully beget offspring.[37] God did not intend us to cohabit via "unwholesome lust."[38] Yet, according to Augustine, in marriage we can and must use the rage of concupiscence for the multiplication of new human beings. If we do not bridle such lust and give in to its cry for mere gratification of self, we will succumb to its evil temptation and become a slave to carnality, thereby losing our sanctity and honor in the manner of those who do not know God.[39]

Quoting the Apostle Paul in I Thessalonians 4:3-5, Augustine urges (male) married Christians to avoid being possessed by carnal concupiscence, the "disease of desire," with all of its raging, inordinate and indecorous motions.[40] Elsewhere in his Book I, Augustine depicts concupiscence as the "wound which the devil has inflicted on the human race" and "the fruit of that ancient stock of pollution" which has been planted in human nature.[41] Concupiscence is not really natural in that it is what God created in us; rather, it is a "corruption" of what is natural in that it is how the devil gains control over us.[42] Since concupiscence arises from sin it is called sin, though in the lives of Christians, those who have been cleansed by the sacrament of regeneration, it is not truly sin, unless the believer allows it to conquer his or her will.[43] If we do allow such uncleanliness to reign in our mortal bodies, our bodies become polluted instruments of unrighteousness.[44] The moral sickness that was remitted in baptism, i.e., forgiven but not eradicated, becomes a current affliction, a bodily "plague," and both the "daughter of sin" and "mother of many sins."[45]

Augustine states further that the wish of baptized Christians "ought to be nothing less that the nonexistence" of concupiscence, "even if the accomplishment of such a wish be not possible in the body of this death."[46] While the believer's task is to avoid willful obedience to fleshly lusts, he or she should seek the compliance of will with divine law, a complete accord gained only when concupiscence is eliminated. For concupiscence is the "languor" of the dis-ease of original sin dwelling within us, urging us to relinquish true, spiritual identity via evil rebellion against the commandments of God (e.g., in covetousness).[47] Concupiscence causes war in the inner self; the Christian should wish for an end to such spiritual aggravation. In the "flesh" there dwells no good thing; its evil desires inhibit the perfection of soul God commands us to have. But as we "find ourselves lying in this diseased state" of concupiscence we may seek "the medicine of Grace" which cures us as we advance in this mortal life toward that future immortality (when perfection can be attained through the banishment of our ultimate sin-sickness, concupiscence).[48] Grace enables the strife-weary believer to delight in divine law, whereby the soul is renewed.[49]

Such renewal, for Augustine, implies a redemption of the body. Citing the Apostle Paul, Augustine notes that concupiscence is the "law of sin" which brings a person into captivity; lusts enslave the body and make it a heavy weight upon the soul. "The body of this death" is taken hostage as a weapon against the Spirit, the true, liberating master of the body (cf. Romans 7:24). But in eternal blessedness with Christ, the body shall live forevermore, "healed of that diseased plague," concupiscence, which presently terrorizes the body.[50] Even now, however, a Christian need not feel guilty about his or her fleshly inclinations, since those who are in Christ Jesus are not indicted for the body's abnormal disease process via concupiscence.[51] Though a believer is born with his or her parents' condition of carnality, upon baptismal regeneration the believer is freed from the guilt of his or her inherited sinful desires. The Christian still lives with the disease of the flesh "derived" from Adam and "contracted" from his or her parents. But redemption is available by way of baptismal "cleansing" and "healing" via sanctifying grace.[52]

In Book II of *On Marriage and Concupiscence,* Augustine is eager to defend Book I against the few, scattered rejoinders of Julian which he has at his disposal. Augustine restates Julian's Pelagian (and, therefore, heretical) designation of a human will that is free enough to do good without God's constantly renewed help; he also refutes Julian's charge that the doctrine of original sin, with its wound of concupiscence, is a Manichaean teaching.[53] Siding with Catholic Christianity, Augustine differentiates his viewpoint from Pelagianism and Manichaeism in the following manner:

> Catholics say that human nature was created good by the
> good God as Creator; but that, having been corrupted by sin,
> it needs the physician Christ. The Manichaeans affirm, that

human nature was not created by God good, and corrupted by sin; but that man was formed by the prince of eternal darkness of a mixture of two natures which had ever existed--one good and the other evil. The Pelagians and Caelestians [i.e., followers of Caelestius, a Pelagian heretic] say that human nature was created good by the good God; but that it is still so sound and healthy in infants at their birth, that they have no need at that age of Christ's medicine.[54]

By identifying his position as Catholic, Augustine sees himself on the side of truth. Regarding human nature, the Manichaeans are wrong, for example, in their denial of a good, almighty Creator God who blesses men and women who unite their flesh in marriage; the Manichaeans unduly censure human nature. The Pelagians, however, hep undue praise upon human nature and claim that even newborn babes have the power to do good without any special, adventitious help from God in Christ. They falsely deny the present dangers of enslaving lust.[55] In short, the Manichaeans see human nature as created both good and evil--the concupiscence within is not a foreign element brought on by inherited sin; the Pelagians, on the other hand, admit the created goodness of human nature, but deny the fact of inherited sin (and, therefore, concupiscence), which makes the Christian life a struggle to be free through grace. Catholics have the true picture of human nature, according to Augustine, because they combine the soul's created goodness, its wound of sin, and its possibility of renewed freedom in grace--all together in one realistic portrayal, in the light of Scriptural authority.

In denying that his perspective is Manichaean, Augustine is able to assert that carnal lust is the only factor in marriage that is of the prince of this world, the devil; concupiscence, once again, comes from sin, not from marriage. Shameful, sexual desire--the mature Augustine's model for lust--is derived from the ancient sin of Adam, which acts as a spoil upon subsequent human nature. In the seminal rebellion of Adam a fault of nature is transmitted and we are all born with a body of death that seeks to live apart form God, via natural appetite.[56] Although sinful lust really belongs to the soul and not the body, we all begin our lives with our bodies captive to sin, which is the devil's creation. But as we receive God's grace we able to start a recovery of our bodies, which are meant to be free vessels of the Spirit. Augustine agrees with many contemporary psychologists and others in that he sees the need "to restore the wounded human soul to wholeness"; yet his recovery process is, of course, "affected only by the grace of God" (Gerald Bonner).[57] Such grace, implanted by baptism, acts upon the human soul so that concupiscence is diminished in favor of a stronger, healthier desire for the Spiritual presence via charity (the true love of God). Augustine disagrees with Julian's view of concupiscence as a gift from heaven; rather, lust is an invention of the devil to control our bodies and, therefore, we must seek continence.[58] God is not the author of such evil lust; indeed, it is God who re-makes us in Christ, who delivers us from the power of darkness.[59] God created human nature and it was good; and while we find it corrupted by Adam's depraved will, the good God sends the merciful Savior to heal it.[60]

The great sin of the first man, Adam, is the cause of our sinful disease of concupiscence, according to Augustine. In following evil persuasion, Adam corrupted his own nature and ours as well, since we all were born in him. He wounded not only himself, but life itself. To describe the universal human affliction brought on by Adam, Augustine uses a medical description:

> This wound was at that fatal moment of the fall inflicted by the devil to a vastly wider and deeper extent than are the sins which are known amongst men. Whence it came to pass, that our nature having then and there been deteriorated by that great sin of the first man, not only was made a sinner, but also generates sinners; and yet the very weakness, under which the virtue of a holy life has drooped and died, is not really nature, but corruption; precisely as a bad state of health is not a bodily substance or nature, but disorder; very often, indeed, if not always, the ailing character of parents is in a certain way implanted, and reappears in the bodies of their children.[61]

In this context, Augustine reaffirms the inbred hurt of all humans which must be cured by a great Physician. In disagreement with the seemingly kinder, gentler doctrine of the Pelagians which sentimentalizes the goodness of newborn children, Augustine asserts that the glorification of infantile innocence may lead us to a wrongful denial of medicine to those who need it most.[62] If children are indeed born into sin and wounded by concupiscence, then we should not deny them the healing of Christ in baptism. We are all in dire need of an antidote for our contracted sin-disease.[63]

ASSESSMENT: CONCUPISCENCE AS ADDICTION

The mature Augustine overplays the role of sinful lust in sexual intercourse. Though he does not identify sex as sin, he comes dangerously close to viewing such a beautiful bodily communication as an inherited moral disease. He does make it clear that God creates and blesses the reproductive process, and that sin is not a biological act; yet he gives the impression that any enjoyment of (even marital) sexual intercourse is sinful.[64] For Augustine, marriage is for procreation, but we are to accomplish such a task willingly and without desire for the flesh. He even comments that, in paradise, before sin existed, sex was possible without the "lascivious heart" of shameful desire.[65] Apparently sexual intercourse as a purely willful, passionless act is Augustine's preference, if we really must do such a thing. Continence, i.e., total abstinence, is the best way to live, but if we cannot ascend to such a lifestyle, we should marry and use lust only as a preparation for procreative acts. If we cannot avoid or eliminate sexual desire in this earthly life, says Augustine, we may as well seek to live with it as a subduable adjunct to conjugal generation of offspring, a necessary evil accompanying lawful cohabitation.[66]

It is not surprising that Augustine's theory provokes strong disagreement. For example, as Paul Lehmann remarks in reference to *On Marriage and Concupiscence:*

> From our perspective, reinforced by medical and psychological sexual research, Augustine seems to be at his worst incontinence is hindered from falling into the ruin of profligacy by the honorable estate of matrimony' stirs up an immediate and strong resentment in the modern mind. No wonder Pelagius found Augustine's whole argument a perverse libel upon human nature and a virtual blasphemy against the divine ordination of marriage so plainly taught in Scripture.[67]

And, as Bonner states:

> On a foundation of physiological fact, erroneously explained, and a sense of shame accurately observed and probably rightly associated with the physiological fact, Augustine rears the structure of his theory of the transmission of Original Sin. Because of the disobedience of our members and the fact of shame, an element has come into human sexuality since the Fall which is both a consequence and a cause of sin. That element is concupiscence or lust. . .But why is it vicious? A question which may particularly be asked today, when a vast quality of literature, of varying degrees of respectability, has grown up on the topic of the

importance of physical satisfaction in marital relationships. Is the pleasure afforded by sexual intercourse in itself any more reprehensible than that given, say, by the enjoyment of good food? Why should one particular pleasure be singled out for rebuke?[68]

Both Lehmann and Bonner are correct in their initial resistance to Augustine's obsession with sexual lust as the encompassing meaning of all inherited sin. As they both imply, Augustine's exaggerated account is at least partially induced by appeals to factual error. We have noted that Augustine, as a Catholic interpreter, claims a realistic portrayal of the plight of human nature, versus the Manichaeans and the Pelagians. But perhaps in his polemics he has a tendency to ground his claims in "the hoary stereotypes of popular opinion," i.e., "facts," based on common "fears and prejudices," the universal truths accepted by the average person (Peter Brown).[69] Thus, for instance, when Augustine points to the shame surrounding the sex act, the social disapproval of reckless sexual passion, or the ways in which people cover their genitals, in support of his exaggerated sense of sexual concupiscence, he shows the weakness of a man who sanctions folk wisdom to protect his stance in public controversy.[70] At times Augustine does seem like a man bent on proving his points of debate by using whatever means he has at his rhetorical disposal.

Perhaps Augustine exaggerates because he wishes to explain the inherent disorder of sinful human life. As an ancient citizen of a declining Roman civilization and a thinking person convinced of the Greek hierarchy of being, Augustine may be obsessed with the ida of sexual lust because he sees in it the most obvious area of human life where desire runs counter to the control of reason.[71] His work, *On Original Sin,* certainly evidences his fear of sexual lust, which he says is due to the beastly side of human nature in conflict with the spiritual purposes of God.[72] For Augustine, "lust rules out moderation," especially in the case of sexual desire (G.R.Evans).[73] And while in *The City of God* he agrees that there are "many different kinds of lust," he focuses on sexual lust as a special sickness of desire which can almost totally extinguish mental alertness and overwhelm "the intellectual sentries."[74] Some have interpreted Augustine as appearing, at times, like an ancient philosopher who believes that the disorderly desires of the body must be tamed to bring a peaceful order to the mind.[75]

Or perhaps Augustine's overemphasis on sexual concupiscence follows from his attachment to Scriptural texts which, in his view, convey the central role of sex as the transmission of sin. For instance, Augustine is first convinced of the transmission of sin through his reading of the Psalms.[76] Psalm 51:5, in particular ("Indeed, I was born guilty, a sinner when my mother conceived me."--The New Revised Standard Version), connects the transmission of sin with natural birth as a result of intercourse. Throughout his writings, Augustine seeks to understand Pauline anthropology in terms of sexual desire as the preeminent force of the flesh which wars against the Spirit (cf. I Corinthians 7; Galatians 5; and especially Romans 5-8). No doubt that Scriptural warrant is an important factor in Augustine's preoccupation with sexual lust as the model for concupiscence. While Scriptural meanings are often transposed to fit his Neoplatonic categories, Augustine finds in the Bible the raw material for his counsel that shameful concupiscence is an inherited sinful orientation which must be dealt with radically.[77] Many times Augustine does narrowly interpret Scripture to justify his exaggeration of the force and significance of sexual lust.

But I suspect that the major motive of Augustine's obsession with sexual lust lies in his own personal experience with what we would now call "sexual addiction."[78] Augustine urges his readers to understand his views within the context of his life; it is clear that his writings give much evidence of his struggle with the flesh in the sexual sphere.[79] For example, Augustine says that in his later youth his life was out of control: "I was tossed about and spilt out in my fornications."[80] Plunged "into a whirlpool of shameful deeds," he "could not distinguish the calm light of chaste love from the fog of lust."[81] He admits in his **Confessions** that sexual lust had restricted his will; he relates how "the fetters of desire for concubinage" made him an "unhappy man."[82] He even gives witness to the addictive process of his past life of sexual concupiscence:

> The enemy [i.e., Satan] had control of my will, and out of it he fashioned a chain and fettered me with it. For in truth lust is made out of a perverse will, and when lust is served, it becomes habit, and when habit is not resisted, it becomes necessity. By such links, joined one to another, as it were-- for this reason I have called it a chain--a harsh bondage held me fast.[83]

Furthermore, Augustine testifies to the "heavy languor" of his problem with sex; like all addicts his compulsive behavior drained his vital energies and left him in spiritual sluggishness.[84] His conversion experience, therefore, woke him up to a new life of freedom through God's grace. It is interesting that the Scriptural passage which Augustine claims gave him so much inner peace at his garden awakening reads as follows: "Let us live honorably as in the day, not in reveling and drunkenness, not in debauchery and licentiousness, not in quarreling and jealousy. Instead, put on the Lord Jesus Christ, and make no provision for the flesh, to gratify its desires" (Romans 13:13-14, NRSV).[85] We must accept the fact that Augustine is well aware of his sex-addiction (or enslavement, as he would call it).[86] While, of course, Augustine casts a quick glance at other types of lust in his theory of concupiscence, he definitely makes sexual desire **the** model for our inherited sin-sickness, to the extent that he can easily substitute the word *libido* of *concupiscentia* in the course of his writings.[87]

I believe that Augustine's preoccupation with the addictive power of sex is due to his wrongful identification of his own experience as the norm for all human experience. Yes, sexual compulsion is a commonly powerful and problematic force. But it is, after all, only one type of addiction which plagues the human race. Indeed, the soul (the real instigator of concupiscent rebellion against the Spirit) can tempt a person in many ways other than through sexual lust.[88] I agree with Bonner when he questions why Augustine must single out sexual pleasure for rebuke. Why not food, alcohol, gambling, shopping, or work addiction? According to many contemporary health care professionals, just about anything or anyone can become an addiction.[89] And there are many addictions which can be "inherited"; studies now abound in reference to the children of addictive families.[90] Chaotic sexual desire is not the only, or necessarily the main, disturber of human nature; nor must it be the only way in which we may receive the dis-ease of original sin from our forebears. Granted, Augustine's exaggeration of sexual concupiscence is useful as a theological precursor to Freudian libido or as a demythologization of our 20th century fascination with romance, "free love," and orgasmic delight.[91] But as a truly general designation for the sum total of our human compulsions, the notion of sexual lust is inadequate.

Yet I contend that Augustine does not exaggerate in his naming corruptive desire per se as an inherited sin-disease which affects all of humanity; as a notion not restricted to sexual lust, but generalized to refer to all our enslaving habits, concupiscence is a properly Christian designation for the moral sickness of compulsiveness which has infected the human race from ancient times. For example, from the vantage point of Scripture, Augustine rightly adduces concupiscence (cf. *epithumia*) to point to our often ruinous preoccupations with the things of this world.[92] As "an intense emotional assertion of the self," concupiscence need not be sinful, as Augustine himself points out, but it often is when it is misdirected or excessive.[93] Disoriented desire, e.g., love of money, produces disharmony (I Timothy 6:9-10); excessive lust ruins human life (Proverbs 1:18; James 4:104). Occasionally, as in

Matthew 5:28, lust is restricted to sexual experience. But usually concupiscent desire is an expression of any human lust gone astray or awry.

In the Pauline descriptions of the "lusts of the flesh," we have an important indication of wayward desire and its effects upon human personality (cf. Romans 8:13-14; Galatians 5:16-23). Augustine is indeed correct in signifying Paul's "ethical" use of the "flesh" (*sarx*) as a reference to our inherited impulse to evil (cf. George E. Ladd).[94] While we must not take *sarx* to mean simply the body or some lower element in the ontology of human being, we also must not limit its desires to the sexual sphere. *Sarx* does not mean sex; it means the whole human person in rebellion against the Spirit of God. *Sarx* does not usually mean the body; but often it does mean the foolish misuse of the body. And *sarx* does not mean our so-called lower physical appetites; but it very well could, at times, refer to our ignoble passions. Mainly, *sarx* means our unregenerate human nature, which gives us trouble as we give our lives over to God, who makes us holy in the Spirit.[95] We must resist the old ascetical tendency to collapse the Pauline moral distinction of flesh and Spirit into a metaphysical dualism of body and soul.[96] More properly understood, the body is a sacred treasure which the flesh attempts to wrest from the Spirit, as a person strives to live righteously under divine law via the sanctifying grace of God in Christ.[97] During the struggle the flesh is a persistent drag which hinders a full development of personhood. As Augustine rightly points out, sinful flesh is a weakness, a death-orientation, inherited from Adam, and persisting even in believers.[98] The essential manifestation of our inbred death inclination is found in the lusts of the flesh, what in a single term may be called concupiscence.[99]

Augustine's notion of concupiscence is not only Scripturally relevant, it is also empirically valuable as a theological description of how humans relate dysfunctionally to the world and to themselves.[100] His perspective on disorderly desire as an inherited sin-sickness helps us to understand that our compulsive behaviors do "not begin with a conscious turning from God," though they are rooted in such a rebellion transmitted to us from ancient times; rather, such destructive processes of habit begin "in an obscure manner" and they are "for long periods more or less unnoticed, being simply implicit in the distortion of our relation to the world and to ourselves" (Wolfhart Pannenberg).[101] In short, we all have a moral illness, brought on ultimately by the Fall; we contract it at birth and we carry it to ourselves and others. This disease is emotional; it is a corruptive desire to relate to the world and ourselves in a deathly fashion. Such an ailment of soul is not a wound that is caused initially by our own crime of rebellion against God and divine creation; we may, of course, become sicker as a result of our own inevitable self-centeredness, e.g., in prideful transgression, but we need to remember that even the worst cases of self=destructive compulsion are not helped by condemnation, or "blaming the victim." The only way in which our sin=disease can be cared for is through a ministry of God's grace; the only way in which we can find a "recovery," or salvation, of self in the midst of such corruption is, of course, through God's grace, a "cure" received only when the self is healed totally at the Eschaton, the Day of the Lord, when all those who trust in the Great Physician will be resurrected (totally recovered).

CONCLUSION

Patrick McCormick has authored a book, *Sin as Addiction,* in which he proposes that we explain the mystery of sin by way of an addiction model.[102] His book is very helpful; in it he outlines some of the traditional notions of sin, critiques them, and then argues "that human sinfulness is a kind of addiction," a "sort of illness" which must elicit a therapeutic rather than a punitive response.[103] His study leans heavily on the insights of contemporary addiction experts in the social sciences and twelve step groups such as Alcoholics Anonymous. My approach, however, has been to look into the Christian tradition and bring forth a resource from Augustine which is Biblically grounded yet relevant to our shared experiences of compulsion. Instead of talking of sin as addiction, I have spoken of addiction as sin, i.e., concupiscence. In the notion of sinful lust we find the theological understanding of the cause of all our enslaving habits. When we think of original sin as transmitted in terms of an "hereditary disease, which weakens and enfeebles our nature, making us spiritually sick and in need of the Divine Physician," we may understand sinful existence as a condition of vulnerability to unhealthy attachments (Bonner).[104] And when we add to such a native form of susceptibility the content of unwholesome desire, the legacy of earthly engagement which our forebears passed on to us from the Fall, we have the pathological way of relating to the world and ourselves which forms the basic model for all our other sick attachments to things and people, substances and processes.[105] We have within us a "wild olive" which can give seed to all sorts of addictive fruits.[106] We have the Addiction of all addictions.

ENDNOTES

1. Gerald Bonner, *St. Augustine of Hippo: Life and Controversies* (London: SCM Press, 1963), p. 401. Cf. Gerald Bonner, *God's Decree and Man's Destiny: Studies on the Thought of Augustine of Hippo* (London: Variorum Reprints, 1987), pp. 303-314.

2. See references by the Apostle Paul in Romans 7; Galatians 5:17; and cf. the books of John and James in *The Holy Bible: The New Revised Standard Version* (New York: Oxford University Press, 1989), passim. Cf. Augustine of Hippo, *Augustine On Romans: Propositions From The Epistle to the Romans and Unfinished Commentary On The Epistle to the Romans,* text and trans. Paula Fredriksen Landes (Chico, California: Scholars Press, 1982), passim. Cf. Margaret R. Miles, *Augustine on the Body* (Missoula, Montana: Scholars Press, American Academy of Religion Dissertation Series 31, 1979), p. 67.

3. See the famous quote by Augustine, "For you have made us for yourself, and our heart is restless until it rests in you," in *The Confessions of St. Augustine,* trans. and ed., John K. Ryan (Garden City, NY: Doubleday and Co., Image Books, 1960), Book I, Chapter 1, p. 43; cf. Book II, Chapters 1 and 2, pp. 65-66.

4. Bonner, *St. Augustine of Hippo,* p. 374ff. Cf. Eugene Portalié, *A Guide to the Thought of Saint Augustine,* trans. Ralph J. Bastian (Westport, Connecticut: Greenwood Press, 1960), p. 208ff.

5. Cf. Eugene TeSelle, *Augustine the Theologian* (New York: Herder and Herder, 1970), p. 318. See the view of Augustine on inherited concupiscence versus the Pelagian view in the study by Paul Rigby, *Original Sin in Augustine's Confessions* (University of Ottawa Press, 1987), p. 70.

6. John J. Hugo, *St. Augustine on Nature, Sex and Marriage* (Chicago: Scepter, 1969), pp. 92-93.

7. Miles, *Augustine on the Body*, p. 70.

8. Augustine of Hippo, *Against Julian,* trans. Matthew A. Schumacher, vol. 35, *The Fathers of the Church* (New York: The Fathers of the Church, Inc., 1957), III (21), Chapter 11, pp. 124-125, and (42), Chapter 21, pp. 144-145.

9. Margaret R. Miles, *Fullness of Life: Historical Foundations for a New Asceticism* (Philadelphia: Westminster Press, 1981), pp. 72, 76.

10. Paul Lehmann, "The Anti-Pelagian Writings," in *A Companion to the Study of St. Augustine,* ed. Roy W. Battenhouse (Grand Rapids, Michigan: Baker Book House, 1979), p. 221.

11. Peter Brown, *Augustine of Hippo: A Biography* (Berkeley, California: University of California Press, 1967), p. 387.

12. Augustine, *Against Julian,* VI (15), Chapter 15, pp. 355-356.   Cf. Augustine of Hippo, *The Trinity,* trans. and ed. John Burnaby, in *Augustine: Later Works* (Philadelphia: Westminster Press, The Library of Christian Classics, Ichthus Edition, 1955) Book IX, 13, p. 66. In this essay I shall leave aside the whole Protestant-Roman Catholic debate on whether or not concupiscence is essentially sin. It is clear, however, that Augustine himself sees concupiscence as **of** sin and **leading** to sin, but not **essentially** sin unless it is obeyed by the human will. See Portalié, *A Guide to the Thought of St. Augustine,* pp. 208-209.

13. See J. P. Kenny, "Concupiscence," in the *New Catholic Encyclopedia,* vol. IV (New York: McGraw Hill, 1967), pp. 121-125.

14. Karl Rahner, *Theological Investigations: God, Christ, Mary and Grace,* vol. I (New York: Crossroad, 1982), p. 360.

15. Hugo, *St. Augustine on Nature, Sex and Marriage,* p. 55.

16. Cf. the notion of *amor* which seeks satisfaction as *concupiscentia* or as *charitas* in J. Burnaby's fourth note on Augustine's terminology in the Introduction to *The Trinity* in Augustine, *Later Works,* pp. 35-36; see Augustine's own words in the same work, Book IX, 13, p. 66. Cf. Augustine's discussion of virtue as "ordered love" (*ordo amoris*) in Augustine, *The City of God,* trans. Henry Bettenson (New York: Penguin Books, 1984), XV, 22, pp. 636-637.

17. Robert J. O'Connell, *St. Augustine's Early Theory of Man, A.D. 386-391* (Cambridge, Massachusetts: Harvard University Press, The Belnap Press, 1968), p. 173. See Augustine of Hippo, *The Free Choice of the Will,* trans. Robert P. Russell, vol. 59, *The Fathers of the Church* (New York: Catholic University of America Press, 1968), I, 8ff., Chapter 3, p. 77.

18. O'Connell, *St. Augustine's Early Theory of Man,* pp. 173-183.

19. Augustine, *Confessions,* Book 3, Chapter 8, p. 88. Cf. Robert J. O'Connell, *St. Augustine's Confessions: The Odyssey of the Soul* (Cambridge, Massachusetts: Harvard University Press, The Belnap Press, 1969), passim. See also Margaret R. Miles, "Infancy, Parenting, and Nourishment in

Augustine's *Confessions,*" *Journal of the American Academy of Religion,* vol. L, No. 3 (1982), pp. 349-364.

20. Miles, *Augustine on the Body,* p. 67.

21. Ibid., pp. 69-70. Cf. references to the debated thesis of Augustine's three-stage development of original sin in his writings via Rigby, *Original Sin in Augustine's Confessions,* p. 28ff. and 69ff.

22. Portalié, *A Guide to the Thought of St. Augustine,* p. 66.

23. Ibid., p. 267. Cf. Augustine of Hippo, *The Good of Marriage* trans. Charles T. Wilcox, vol. 27, *The Fathers of the Church* (New York: The Fathers of the Church, Inc., 1955), pp. 9-51.

24. Augustine, *The Good of Marriage,* (5), Chapter 6, p. 17ff.

25. Ibid., (9), Chapter 9, p. 22.

26. For an overview of Julian's charges of Manichaeism versus Augustine, see Brown, *Augustine of Hippo,* p. 370 and p. 386ff.

27. Bonner, *St. Augustine of Hippo,* p. 154.

28. See "From the Preface of Augustine's 'Unfinished Work Against Julianus'" in *The Nicene and Post-Nicene Fathers,* vol. V, ed. Philip Schaff (Grand Rapids: Michigan: Wm. B. Eerdmans, 1956), p. 281.

29. Ibid., fn. 2. Cf. Bonner, *God's Decree and Man's Destiny,* XII, p. 157, 160.

30. Augustine of Hippo, *On Marriage and Concupiscence,* trans. Peter Holmes and Robert E. Wallis, vol. V, *Nicene and Post-Nicene Fathers,* Book I, Chapter 1, p. 264.

31. Ibid.

32. Ibid., Chapters 3-5, pp. 264-265.

33. Ibid., Chapter 5, p. 265.

34. Ibid., Chapter 6, p. 265; chapter 19, p. 271; and Chapter 23, p. 273.

35. Ibid., Chapter 8, p. 267.

36. Ibid.

37. Ibid., Chapter 7, p. 266.

38. Ibid., Chapter 9, p. 267.

39. Ibid.

40. Ibid. Cf. Book II, Chapter 55, p. 306.

41. Ibid., Chapter 26, p. 274. Cf. Bonner, *God's Decree and Man's Destiny,* p. 310. Cf. Augustine of Hippo, *Against Two Letters of the Pelagians,* in vol. V, *Nicene and Post-Nicene Fathers,* I 13, 27.

42. Ibid.

43. Ibid., Chapter 25, p. 274.

44. Ibid. Cf. Romans 6:12, 13.

45. Ibid., Chapters 27, 28 and 35, pp. 275, 278.

46. Ibid., Chapter 30, p. 276. Cf. Romans 7.

47. Ibid., Chapters 30-31, p. 276, and Chapter 28, p. 275.

48. Ibid., Chapter 32, p. 276.

49. Ibid., Chapter 33, p. 277.

50. Ibid., Chapter 35, p. 278.

51. Ibid., Chapter 36, p. 278.

52. Ibid., Chapter 37, pp. 278-279.

53. Augustine, *On Marriage and Concupiscence,* Book II, Chapter 8, pp. 285-286.

54. Ibid., Chapter 9, p. 286.

55. Ibid.

56. Ibid., Chapters 11-16, pp. 287-289.

57. Bonner, *God's Decree and Man's Destiny*, p. 314.

58. Augustine, *On Marriage and Concupiscence*, Book II, Chapter 23, pp. 291-292.

59. Ibid., Chapter 33, p. 296.

60. Ibid., Chapter 34, pp. 297-298, and chapter 48, p. 302.

61. Ibid., Chapter 57, p. 307.

62. Ibid., Chapter 56, p. 307, and Chapter 60, p. 308.

63. Ibid., Chapter 58, p. 307.

64. Ibid., Chapter 14, p. 288.

65. Ibid., Chapter 13, p. 287, and Chapter 26, p. 293. Cf. Augustine, *City of God*, XIV, 16, p. 577.

66. Augustine, *On Marriage and Concupiscence*, Book I, Chapter 5, p. 265, and Chapter 9, p. 267.

67. Lehmann, in *A Companion to the Study of St. Augustine*, p. 221. Cf. Augustine, *On Marriage and Concupiscence*, Book I, Chapter 18, p. 271. Cf. I Corinthians 7:2.

68. Bonner, *St. Augustine of Hippo*, p. 375. Note that Augustine says he has problems with food also--cf. his *Confessions*, Book 10, Chapter 31, pp. 257-260.

69. Brown, *Augustine of Hippo*, p. 389.

70. Ibid. Cf. Augustine, *On Marriage and Concupiscence*, Book I, Chapter 8, p. 266, and Chapter 24, p. 274. Cf. Augustine, *Against Julian*, IV (59), Chapter 12, pp. 217-219. Cf. Augustine, *City of God*, XIV, 17, pp. 578-579.

71. TeSelle, *Augustine the Theologian*, pp. 316-317.

72. Augustine of Hippo, *On Original Sin,* trans. Peter Holmes and Robert E. Wallis, in vol. V, *Nicene and Post-Nicene Fathers,* Chapter 41, p. 252, and Chapter 46, p. 254. Cf. Augustine, *On Marriage and Concupiscence,* Book II, Chapter 14, p. 24.

73. G. R. Evans, *Augustine on Evil* (Cambridge: Cambridge University Press, 1982), p. 163.

74. Augustine, *City of God,* XIV, Chapter 16, p. 577.

75. See Evans, *Augustine on Evil,* pp. 163-164. Yet we must be careful to note that, for Augustine, lust disturbs the will, which is more than intellect. As the integrating force of human personality, will includes intellect but it is not limited to such.

76. TeSelle, *Augustine the Theologian,* p. 316.

77. Thomas J. Bigham and Albert T. Mollegen, "The Christian Ethic," in Battenhouse, ed., *A Companion to the Study of St. Augustine,* p. 382.

78. Cf. Patrick Carnes, *Out of the Shadows* (Minneapolis: CompCare, 1988), passim. See also his more recent work, *Don't Call It Love: Recovery From Sexual Addiction* (New York: Bantam Books, 1991), passim. Cf. Linda K. Inman and Margaret Heath Donahue, "Sexual Addiction--Don't Call It Love: An Interview with Patrick Carnes," in *New England Journey,* May, 1991, pp. 1, 13.

79. See Augustine, *Confessions,* Books 2-8, pp. 65-203. Cf. Miles, "Infancy, Parenting, and Nourishment in Augustine's *Confessions,*" p. 358.

80. Ibid., Book 2, Chapter 2, p. 66.

81. Ibid., Book 2, Chapter, p. 65.

82. Ibid., Book 8, Chapters 5 and 6, p. 190.

83. Ibid., Book 8, Chapter 5, pp. 188-189.

84. Ibid., Book 8, Chapter 5, p. 189.

85. Ibid., Book 8, Chapter 12, p. 202.

86. Miles, *Fullness of Life*, pp. 72, 77.

87. Bonner, *God's Decree and Man's Destiny*, p. 304ff.

88. TeSelle, *Augustine the Theologian*, p. 317. Cf. Peter Brown, *Augustine and Sexuality*, ed. Mary Ann Donovan (Berkeley, California: Colloquy 46, The Center for Hermeneutical Studies in Hellenistic and Modern Culture, 1983), p. 4.

89. See, for example, Gerald May, *Addiction and Grace* (San Francisco: Harper and Row, 1988), pp. 37-39.

90. Cf. Craig Nakken, *The Addictive Personality: Understanding Compulsion in Our Lives* (San Francisco: Harper and Row, Hazeldon Books, 1988), pp. 73-87.

91. Hugo, *St. Augustine on Nature, Sex and Marriage*, pp. 93-105.

92. Kenneth Grayston, "Desire," in *A Theological Word Book of the Bible*, ed. Alan Richardson (New York: Macmillan Co., 1950), p. 64.

93. Ibid.

94. George E. Ladd, *A Theology of the New Testament* (Grad Rapids, Michigan: Wm B. Eerdmans, 1974), p. 473.

95. Ibid., pp. 466-474.

96. Miles, *Fullness of Life*, p. 158.

97. Ibid.

98 Augustine, *Propositions from the Epistle to the Romans, in Augustine on Romans*, Proposition 26ff., p. 9ff.

99. For warnings against concupiscent desire and lists of accompanying vices, see the following Scripture texts: Titus 3:3; I Peter 4:3; Colossians 3:5; Romans 1:24-27 and 13:14; Ephesians 2:3; and throughout II Peter and James.

100. Wolfhart Pannenberg, *Anthropology in Theological Perspective*, trans. Matthew J. O'Connell (Philadelphia: Westminster Press, 1985), pp. 91-96.

101. Ibid., p. 94.

102. Patrick McCormick, *Sin as Addiction* (New York: Paulist Press, 1989), passim. Cf. J. Keith Miller, *A Hunger for Healing: The Twelve Steps as a Classic Model for Christian Spiritual Growth* (San Francisco: HarperCollins, 1991), pp. 1-30. See also Meredith B. Handspicker, "Addiction: A Review Article," *Andover Newton Review,* vol. 1, No. 1 (Spring 1990), pp. 37-39.

103. Ibid., p. 146ff.

104. Bonner, *St. Augustine of Hippo,* p. 371.

105. Cf. McCormick, *Sin as Addiction,* p. 150. See Nakken, *The Addictive Personality,* p. 10. See also Anne Wilson Schaef, *When Society Becomes An Addict* (San Francisco: Harper and Row, 1987), p. 18ff.

106. Augustine, *On Marriage and Concupiscence,* Book I, Chapter 21, p. 272.

CHAPTER TWO

ON LANGUAGE AND GOD

John David (Jack) Graham
Earlham School of Religion

ABSTRACT

God is neither male nor female; but male language for God
is a theological necessity for anything else would alter the
salvific nature of God.

In her book, *The Divine Feminine,* Virginia Mollenkott tells the story of the
Peanuts cartoon character, Snoopy, who is laboriously trying to produce an
article called "Beauty Tips." Triumphantly he concludes it by referring to the
sage advice, "Always remember that beauty is only skin deep," only to realize
on closer personal inspection that "fur deep" would be more appropriate. The
next day, however, he is visited by Woodstock, his bird friend, who offers him
strong advice concerning his article. As a result, Snoopy changes his
conclusion to read "feather deep." That, according to Mollenkott, is the
essence of the feminist argument for a change in our language on an earthly
level when referring to one another and on a heavenly scale when referring
to God; for anything short of a totally inclusive vocabulary would theologically
exclude all the "beagles and birds" of our society.[1]

Unfortunately, according to Mollenkott, this is precisely what has happened
to women who have been excluded both vocationally and salvifically by
traditional Christian teachings, as a visit to almost any church on Sunday
morning will indicate. Considering the fact that just minor manipulation of
grammar will open, not only vocations, but salvation, to over half of our
society now excluded, it is, therefore, her contention that particularly when in
reference to God, the use of "gender sensitive" language is a necessity for the
spiritual good of all.[2]

The danger, particularly in reference to God-language, as Kathleen Fischer states in *Women At The Well,* is that the exclusive use of male metaphors, and especially that of Father, runs the risk of idolatry by confusing the human symbol with the divine reality. In other words, the exclusive use of male God-language restricts the religious experience of all believers, and especially that of women.[3] As Carol Christ suggests, "Women can never have the experience that is freely available to every many and boy in her culture, of having her full sexual identity affirmed as being in the image and likeness of God".[4] She concludes by saying that as a consequence, it is difficult for a woman to believe deeply in her own sacredness, her own power, and her own capacity to image the divine. Thus it is no wonder that many women struggle throughout life with feelings of low self-worth.[5]

It is Fischer's contention that the male concept of God, although perceived as theological, is not at root a theological issue. Rather it is a sociological one for there is a reciprocal relationship between language and experience. That is, images of God that are perceived as domineering tend to create a hierarchical structure for women in relation to men and to God, and that is both physically and spiritually demeaning. For example, even the terms such as Judge, King, Lord, and assorted other "masculine themes" come into question because of the socially and spiritually repressive images they present for women.[6] It is her contention that women should instead establish a relationship of "cooperation" with God; one in which God moves "down" and they move "up"[7] and where they no longer see themselves as a mere child.[8] Thus there is a genuine awareness of their own authority and no longer the "up-down" relationship of God as Father, Judge, Lord and such related images.[9]

Rosemary Ruether in *Sexism and God-Talk,* agrees with Fischer that the God-language issue is not at root a theological one. Rather than seeing it as rooted in sociological relationships as Fischer does, she sees it as rooted in history and merely expressed in sociological relationships. Her contention is that to bring modern women into full equality, both physically and spiritually, we must reach back behind patriarchal monotheism to the religions in which a goddess was either the dominant divine image or was paired with a divine male image.[10]

Ruether asserts that based on the archeological evidence available to us today, it appears that the most ancient image of the divine was female. Quoting E.O. James book, *The Cult of the Mother Goddess,* she states that "the mother-goddess cult must indeed be one of the oldest and longest surviving religions of the ancient world".[11] The figures of the goddess typically emphasized the breasts, buttocks and enlarged abdomen of the female, with little attention given to the face, hands and legs. This suggests, she says, that the goddess was not a focus of personhood, but rather an "impersonalized image of the mysterious powers of fecundity (fertility).[12] This pregnant human female thus was the central metaphor of life giving power for a people totally dependent on that power for survival. These people did not visualize themselves as controlling the life process, but rather as cooperating with it. Thus by shaping and even burying these images of fertility in an effort to induce the fertility of the earth, they were, in one sense, co-creating with the goddess in the renewal of life each spring. this image, despite centuries of male monotheism, is still maintained in modern society with metaphors for the divine as "Ground of Being" and even "Mother Earth".[13]

In later Sumerian and Babylonian civilizations, this "earth force" goddess had not only taken on more typically human features, but a male consort as well. With two gods, a male and female, the annual fertility of the earth each spring and the religious rites that were designed to induce it, called sympathetic magic, were now more closely aligned with that of the human reproductive act. Thus as the female gave birth to new life which was a part of her, so too, did the earth goddess give birth to the universe and its inhabitants which were then a part of the goddess. Therefore, as the creator was divine, the creation was divine also.[14]

It is Ruether's contention that based on this historical argument, one that predates that of the hierarchical male structure of the Judeo-Christian Godhead, the gods and goddesses of the ancients, and thus the human structures that were based on the divine structure, were not hierarchical, but rather equivalent, and even co-creating.[15] She contends that male monotheism does not have the historical precedent that the goddess imagery has. It is, in fact, a departure from all precious human consciousness, and one that falsely creates a God-male-female order where women no longer stand in relation to God; one where they are connected secondarily to God through the male.[16]

It is at this point, that of the sociological results of male monotheism, that Ruether and Fischer agree. And it is at this point also, that we must ask the question that is the focus of this paper: are Ruether and Fischer correct in their assumption that the nature of the God-language debate is not theological at root?

According to Elizabeth Achtemeir in her essay, "Female Language For God: Should The Church Adopt It?" contrary to the notion popularized by feminists, the whole issue of God-language is not merely one of semantics, but rather one of theology for several reasons. First and foremost, when female terminology is used for God, the birthing image becomes inevitable. Two examples of this are 1) Naomi Janowitz and Maggie Wening's, "Sabbath "Prayer for Jewish Women: "Blessed is She who spoke and the world became. Blessed is She. Blessed is She who in the beginning, gave birth....Blessed is She whose womb covers the earth..." and 2) Virginia Mollenkott: "We are only reclaiming our biblical and cultural heritage when we see that origin not in terms of masculine impregnation, but rather in terms of feminine involvement in the birth and nurturing process".[17]

Secondly, if we allow the premise that the creator does, in fact, give birth to the creation, then it follows logically that this creation is divine also.[18] As Zsuzsanna E. Budapest states, "We do give birth, we do issue forth people, just as the Goddess issues forth the universe. That is the biological connection and manifestation of the Goddess...And the responsibility you accept is that you are divine, and that you have power".[19] Carol Christ also makes the same assertion when she states that "The woman who says 'I found God in myself and I loved her fiercely,' is saying, '...that the divine principle, the saving and sustaining power, is in herself..." Even Starhawk, who writes out of the pagan context of modern witchcraft reaches this same conclusion: "There is no dichotomy between spirit and flesh, no split between Godhead and the world...Thou art Goddess. I am Goddess".[20]

Thirdly, if humans (and particularly human females) are divine, then there can be no sin on their part.[21] Dorothee Sollee rejects the biblical concept of a "fall" from sinlessness with her rejection of the Adam/Eve story as a concept of original sin, and instead sees it as a form of liberation. "Coming out is liberation. Let us read the story of Adam and Eve as a coming out. The first human beings come out and discover themselves; they discover the joy of learning, the pleasures of beauty and knowledge. Let us praise Eve, who brought this about".[22] Sollee then takes her rejection of sin to its logical conclusion by then rejecting God. "To live, we do not need what has repeatedly been called 'God.' a power that intervenes, rescues, judges and confirms. The most telling argument against our traditional God is not that he no longer exists or that he has drawn back within himself, but that we no longer need him".[23]

Finally, the ultimate deduction for the feminist position is that since there is no sin, there is no need for salvation through Jesus Christ. Salvation, in fact, is restructured in terms of liberation from male oppression or patriarchal tradition. It is found in a discovery and celebration womanhood and human potential. Jesus Christ is then seen as only a prophet offering enlightened views on human relations, often defined in terms of some androgynous ideal.[24] Sheila Collins states that "salvation is the discovery and celebration of the 'other' in ourselves. When men discovery their femininity and women their masculinity, then perhaps we can form a truly liberating and mutually enriching partnership".[25]   Even Matthew Fox cites with approval the pseudepigraphal Gospel of Thomas: "Until you make the male female and the female male, you will not enter the kingdom".[26]

There is no doubt that sociologically both Fischer and Ruether are correct is stating that society in general, and the church in particular, has discriminated against women by denying ordination, leadership, influence, status, and at times, even participation in the life of the Body of Christ based solely on their biology. There is also no doubt that the gospel is at heart a rejection of that vocational, emotional and spiritual bondage. Yet unlike Fischer, Ruether and a host of other feminists who justify the revision of the God-language based on this injustice, it is the position of this paper that this issue, although expressed and even fought in the sociological arena through the use of linguistic manipulation, is at heart a theological one whose intent is not a relationship with God, but rather a substantive alteration of our understanding of God.

Rosemary Ruether was correct in stating that the Hebrew culture was unlike any other in history with its use of the decidedly masculine pronouns for God. she was not correct, however, in suggesting that this was a flaw in their culture that needs to b corrected in ours. As our discussion clearly shows, the reasoning for this pronoun use was not designed for the subjection of one gender to another, but rather that we would never lose sight of the fact that we are exactly what Scripture calls us, God's creation; not god's; not even co-creating with God; but simply God's creation. The feminist theology concerning the feminization of God, if followed to its logical conclusion, will ultimately lead us back to Genesis 3 in a vain attempt to once again "be like God." The true liberation that all people seek, feminists included, is not to found in mere linguistic manipulation. That freedom is today found as it was three=thousand years ago for the Hebrews, our spiritual ancestors, in a personal covenant relationship with our Creator. Anything short of that is, at best, a salvation by semantics.

ENDNOTES

1. Virginia Mollenkott, *The Divine Feminine* (New York: Crossroad, 1988), p. 1.

2. **Ibid.**

3. Kathleen Fischer, *Women at the Well* (New York: Paulist Press, 1988), p. 53.

4. **Ibid.**

5. **Ibid.**

6. **Ibid.,** p. 55.

7. **Ibid.,** p. 57.

8. **Ibid.,** p. 58.

9. **Ibid.,** p. 61.

10. Rosemary Ruether, *Sexism and God-Talk* (Boston: Beacon Press, 1983), p. 47.

11. **Ibid.**

12. **Ibid.,** p. 48.

13. **Ibid.**

14. **Ibid.,** p. 51.

15. **Ibid.,** p. 52.

16. **Ibid.,** p. 53.

17. Elizabeth Achtemeir, "Female Language for God: Should the Church Adopt it?" *The Hermeneutical Quest* (New York: Pickwick Publ., 19986), p. 100.

18. **Ibid.**

19. **Ibid.**, p. 1010.

20. **Ibid.**

21. **Ibid.**, p. 107.

22. **Ibid.**

23. **Ibid.**, p. 108.

24. Donald Bloesch, *Is the Bible Sexist?* (Westchester, IL: Crossway Books, 1982), p. 19.

25. **Ibid.**

26. **Ibid.**

BIBLIOGRAPHY

Achtemeir, Elizabeth. "Female Language for God: Should the Church Adopt it?" *The Hermeneutical Quest.* 1986, Pickwick Publications.

Bloesch, Donald. *Is the Bible Sexist?*, Westchester, Illinois: Crossway Books, 1982.

Fischer, Kathleen. *Women at the Well,* New York: Paulist Press, 1988.

Mollenkott, Virginia. *The Divine Feminine,* New York: Crossroad, 1988.

Ruether, Rosemary. *Sexism and God-Talk,* Boston, Beacon Press: 1983.

CHAPTER THREE

THOSE DAMNED PACIFISTS: On the Horns of Niebuhr's Dilemma

Mark K. Nation
Christian Theological Seminary

ABSTRACT

Reinhold Niebuhr has posed a false dilemma for Christian pacifists. In challenging his approach, I open up the possibility of a broader, and fairer, understanding of Christian pacifism.

INTRODUCTION: The Horns of the Dilemma

James Childress has said that Reinhold Niebuhr often attempted to provide his opponents with only two options: "He would describe his opponents' positions in general terms and try to offer them the horns of a dilemma."[1] I have come to believe that this *modus operandi* is a key to understanding Niebuhr's critique of pacifism. Pacifists who care about the world are, according to Niebuhr, on the horns of a dilemma. On the one side is the law of love, the ideal. On the other side are the ambiguities, the sinful relativities of history. One cannot both embody the ideal (to the point of being absolutely committed to nonviolence) and be involved in any significant way in the relativities of history. There are two ways to resolve the dilemma according to Niebuhr.

First, one can embrace the ideal of nonresistance. Those who have embraced this position historically have been members of Protestant sects or ascetic monastic communities. Often people within this group have had the perfect, selfless, nonresistant love of Jesus as their model. Niebuhr expresses appreciation for these people.[2] For him they represent the ideal of love. They remind all of us that we fall short of the law of love. However, it is important that these people realize that they have forsaken any significant involvement in or responsibility for the world. Their relationship with society is basically a parasitic one.[3]

The alternative way of resolving the dilemma is to renounce an absolute commitment to nonviolence and embrace the historical relativities and concomitant sin of the world. That does not mean that the ideal of selfless love cannot continue to function somewhat as a discriminating principle causing us to care always about pursuing a more perfect justice in the world. However, we will have no illusions about embodying or achieving perfect, selfless love as we participate responsibly in shaping the social and political realities of the world.

Niebuhr will not countenance what he considers to be an illegitimate third approach to resolving the dilemma. This is the claim that it is possible to hold to an absolute commitment to nonviolence while being significantly involved in the relativities of history. Pacifists, Niebuhr claims, cannot have it both ways. To be engaged in the relativities of history is, by definition, to be involved in coercion and the employment of power and, thereby, to abandon the selfless, nonresistance of Jesus.

The questions to be asked of any proposed dilemma are: is it an actual dilemma or is this supposed dilemma more the product of the way things are defined than the actual situation? I will argue that Niebuhr's way of defining the dilemma has predetermined the outcome to suit his polemical purposes more than it has clarified the actual ethical situation.

From the pacifists' own perspective Niebuhr has created a no win situation. They are damned if they do (get involved in social and political realities because they must renounce their commitment to nonviolence). And they are damned if they don't (get involved in social and political issues because they become irresponsible and parasitic). But it is quite possible that there are other ways out of Niebuhr's dilemma.

TYPOLOGIES OF PACIFISM AND THEIR IMPORTANCE FOR NIEBUHR

Pacifism is not one issue among many for Niebuhr. John H. Yoder has stated that for Niebuhr, "...restructuring of theology around the issue of violence and war was at the center of his entire enterprise. The entire theology of Niebuhr is unfolded backwards from his outgrowing of pacifism."[4] Whether or not one would want to put it quite that strongly, there is no question but that much of Niebuhr's writing centered around war and peace, violence and nonviolence, and justice and injustice. And in all of his major writings where he dealt with these subjects it was against the backdrop of a pacifist alternative.

When Niebuhr discusses pacifism he basically has in mind two types. First, and most often, he has in mind the liberal, naive, optimistic kind that he flirted with up to approximately 1932. This variety he has nothing but disdain for. The second type of pacifism he has in mind is the sectarian or ascetic nonresistance. As stated above, this position he has respect for as long as its adherents admit their irrelevance to the larger society. Niebuhr also has appreciation for a Gandhian type of pragmatic nonviolence. However, he does not want it to be categorized as pacifism. Though Niebuhr expresses appreciation for those who, by his definition, are truly nonresistant, it is faint praise from someone who places so much value on active involvement in the larger society--thus his reference to these people as being societal parasites. And yet he defines things in such a way that a pacifist cannot remain pacifist and truly engage the large society responsibly.

As mentioned earlier, it is clear that when Niebuhr thought of pacifist alternatives he thought mainly of his own previous pacifism, a pacifism rooted in a kind of optimism and liberal orientation that he came to reject with avengence. Moreover, a part of the visceral power of Niebuhr's critique of pacifism was the fact that he had been one. However a couple of things should be kept in mind. First, though it cannot be pursued here, it must be noted that there is no written evidence that Niebuhr ever had any carefully developed pacifism--naive, liberal or otherwise. It may well be, as both John Bennett and Ronald Stone have stated, that Niebuhr was never really an absolute pacifist.[5] And, furthermore, even if he was a pacifist, he was a pacifist of a particular type, a type that historically has had few adherents in the Church and has few adherents today.[6]

I should also mention that the way in which I will critique Niebuhr in this paper is based centrally, at least, on a particular type of pacifism, one that John Yoder has labeled "the pacifism of the messianic community."[7] For the sake of brevity in this paper I will refer to this type of pacifism as christological pacifism. Niebuhr would have received a different type of scrutiny under the evaluation of a different type of pacifism. If I had more space I would also mention a number of points at which I agree with and appreciate Niebuhr.

JESUS AND THE IMPOSSIBLE IDEAL

First, in my critique, I will look at Niebuhr's views about Jesus as they relate to pacifism. As was mentioned earlier, Niebuhr believed that the Jesus of the Gospels was a pacifist of a certain type, viz. nonresistant.

> It is very foolish to deny that the ethic of Jesus is an absolute and uncompromising ethic [implying nonresistance]....Nothing is more futile and pathetic than the effort of some Christian theologians who find it necessary to become involved in the relativities of politics, in resistance to tyranny or in social conflict, to justify themselves by seeking to prove that Christ was also involved in some of these relativities, that he used whips to drive the money-changers out of the Temple, or that he came 'not to bring peace but a sword'....[8]

Jesus was not only not involved in such "relativities" of history; he was uninterested in them, according to Niebuhr. "He was not [e.g.] particularly interested in the Jewish people's aspirations toward freedom from Rome, and skillfully evaded the effort to make him take sides in that political problem."[9] And it is not just violent actions that would not be supported by Jesus but there is also "...not the slightest support in Scripture for this doctrine of nonviolence."[10]

There are several things to say about Niebuhr's portrayal of his apolitical, nonresistant Jesus. Of course, my comments on this complicated subject have to be merely suggestive. It may be true, and I would argue that it is, that exegetically it is difficult to derive a violent Jesus from the gospels. However, to move from there to argue that Jesus was uninterested in or uninvolved in the relativities of history is simply not accurate. I would argue rather that we should always be cautious about going to the Scriptures with our modern agenda and then expect to find responses that would fit our expectations. This is true in regards to politics as well. (Although Richard Cassidy has shown that, if done with care, even modern political agenda taken to the gospels can produce some fruit.)[11]

If we seriously want to know how it might have looked for a Palestinian Jew like Jesus to be concerned about and even involved in political matters then we need to be attentive to the political, cultural, and religious situation that obtained in Palestine at the time of Jesus. It might make some sense of his relative silence regarding Rome, e.g., if we took seriously the statement, "I was sent to the lost sheep of the house of Israel, and to them alone." (Mtt. 15.24)

It might make Jesus look less apolitical if we realized that in ancient Israel politics and religion, in most situations, were inseparable--rendering, e.g., the conflicts between Jesus and some of the religious leaders political as well as religious.   But, as I've said, these brief comments can only be suggestive. Marcus Borg has developed them at some length.[12]

What seems clear to me is that the Jesus of the gospels is not some cardboard character that represents an abstract, disembodied ideal of love. He was a real person engaging the real world. The cleansing of the temple might not violate the tenets of pacifism as I understand them but it does not fit a passive, uninvolved, nonresistant image. Neither do the numerous conflicts between Jesus and various leaders in Judea.

What also seems clear to me is that Jesus did embody a perfect, selfless love. Therefore, The Jesus of the gospels begins to loosen the tight vise-grip hold Niebuhr's "dilemma" has on the possibility of holding together a commitment to nonviolence and active concern for the world. IF being involved in the relativities of history automatically involves one in sin then Jesus was sinful. But the New Testament and Christian orthodoxy claim he was without sin. I would also argue that being involved in the relativities of history did not cause Jesus to renounce his commitment to nonviolence, despite Niebuhrs' proposed dilemma.

THOSE WHO WOULD FOLLOW JESUS

But even if an interlocutor were to grant that perhaps Niebuhr has charac-teured Jesus, Jesus' ability to pull off an almost impossible feat is not the same as sinful humans doing it. That is certainly true. However, that does not mean it cannot be done with some degree of success. As in everything else, so here, in attempting to embody the love of Christ, we sinful humans would fall short. But our lack of perfection does not excuse us from pursuing the faithfulness to which God calls us. Christian pacifists would argue that this is true in relation to loving enemies as well as neighbors (and the corollary commitment to nonviolence) as well as in other matters.

In some ways Niebuhr is stereotypically Lutheran. He seems not to be able to write in any sustained way about concepts such as enabling grace and sanctification. Even when he seems to promise such discussions, he ends up engaging in more railing against moralism, legalism, perfectionism, and absolutism.[13]   His reading of Paul, justification by faith, and "legalistic" Judaism would find rough sailing in today's scholarly waters.[14]   This scholarship notwithstanding, I'm convinced, that many still view "sectarians" and pacifists through the kinds of stereotypes Niebuhr presents.

Because this way of looking at pacifists is far from dead I must discuss Niebuhr's use of words like perfectionism, moralism, legalism, and absolutism. These are all loaded terms that serve more to obscure than clarify the discussion through another false set of alternatives. It is only possible here to respond briefly to each term.

First, absolutism. It is simply true that everyone has values and commitments that function for him or her as absolutes. For most people there are few of them: family, integrity of the nation-state, justice, peace, God, Jesus, etc. Logically there is no reason why this sort of commitment is peculiar to pacifists.[15] In fact, one can argue that, "There is nothing more absolute than the claim that it is my business to terminate someone else's life."[16] And for a Christological pacifist the commitment is not to the absence of overt violence but rather to the Lordship of Jesus. It has yet to be explained convincingly why Christians who profess the Lordship of Jesus often feel no need to take Jesus seriously when he says that his followers are to love their enemies as well as their neighbors. (Mtt. 5.38ff.)

I will respond to the other three terms, perfectionism, moralism, and legalism together. Again Niebuhr has used extreme terms in order to evade the deeper moral claims of the pacifist. I would never deny that there have been (and are) some pacifists who are overly rigid, literalistic, and unimaginative in their attempts to be like Jesus. And I would never deny that some have been self-righteous. (A temptation with which all of us must wrestle.) Some of them may have even thought they could be morally perfect or that they could earn their salvation through exhibiting morally righteous behavior (though I have never met such people).

However, to write as if a genuine concern for righteousness and faithfulness is by definition to engage in one or all three of these ""isms" is simply disingenuous. Let me use the analogy of marriage. Within a marriage covenant I should properly be concerned about righteousness and faithful-ness--being a good husband--as that is defined by the covenant and relation-ship. There are a few acts that are clearly defined as violating the covenant, such as adultery and physical abuse. As the relationship continues there grows a complex configuration of appropriate loving deeds as well as deeds that would erode the relationship and covenant. To refuse to engage in the acts that I know violate the covenant is not legalism. Neither is paying attention to the many other deeds that I have learned are expressions of faithfulness and righteousness as defined by our covenant and relationship. All of these acts are the expression of a love and commitment that are appropriate to faithfulness and righteousness as defined by the relationship. And, of course, in a healthy relationship the deeds are not done primarily because they will benefit me. However, if I cannot prove at any given moment that my motives are totally selfless it does not nullify my love for my wife nor does it justify the lowering of my standards for serving her. It simply means I am human and less than perfect.

All of this applies analogously to the pacifist. The pacifist need not be self-righteous, rigid, or moralistic. However, there is a legitimate concern to be faithful to the claim that Jesus is Lord, and to live accordingly. That can be stated in various ways. Stan Hauerwas, a Christological pacifist, refers to living into the story of Jesus: "...to be a Christian is not principally to obey certain commandments or rules, but to learn to grow into the story of Jesus as the form of God's kingdom".[17]

THE FIRST STEP IN CHRISTIAN SOCIAL ETHICS: The Church

It is interesting that there is basically no doctrine of the Church in Niebuhr's writings. He mentions the Church from time to time in passing but it does not figure into his ethics in any substantive way. Some might defend Niebuhr by repeating his claim that he was not a theologian. However, that will not do. To begin with, he slips occasionally and refers to what he is writing as theology.[18] Many of those who have written about his thought refer to him as a theologian. And, furthermore, he was clearly writing theological ethics. If the church did figure into his ethic in any significant way it would be obvious. But it doesn't. This is probably not unrelated to the fact that, as I mentioned earlier, Niebuhr has no substantive concept of enabling grace.

Though I do not have space here to develop it, for some, especially Christological, pacifists this is a serious omission. It is the enabling grace of God and the power of the Holy Spirit that enable Christians to be, however imperfectly, what they are called to be in Christ. And it is because of the transforming and enabling power of God that a new community is created called the Church. As Hauerwas puts it, "Through the story of Jesus I can increasingly learn to be what I have become, a participant in God's community of peace and justice. Only by growing into that story do I learn how much violence I have stored in my soul, a violence which is not about to vanish overnight, but which I must continually work to recognize and lay down."[19]

The Church provides a community of support rooted in common traditions, beliefs, and practices to make greater faithfulness more possible. In addition, this Church as a new creation and a social body is called to be the just and peaceful body of Christ within society. That is to say it is not just that the people within the Church have a social ethic but that the Church itself is a social ethic.[20] But such a conviction requires a substantive concept of both enabling grace and the Church.

A NECESSARY DETOUR REGARDING TERMS

Before I enter into a discussion of how a Christian pacifist might think about involvement in the social and political realm there are two preliminary matters that need to be touched upon. Both relate to vocabulary. Both matters are central to a fair assessment of Niebuhr's understanding and critique of pacifism.

The first relates to Niebuhr's use of the words coercion, power, force, violence, and nonviolence. Niebuhr uses these words inconsistently and with carelessness. I can't decide whether this sloppy use is due mostly to poor scholarship, changing uses to suite various apologetic purposes, or specious argumentation. I tend to think that Niebuhr is guilty of all three. And it does not serve the truth in either case.

To categorize Gandhi's actions with any and all other coercive actions because the significant difference between actions is whether they are coercive or not seems to muddy rather than clarify the discussion. For Niebuhr to suggest that making an absolute distinction between violence and non-violence is to group a Goebbels with a Gandhi is tendentious.[21] Of course, in a narrow, literalistic sense many of Goebbels' activities were nonviolent. But no one would have seriously suggested that Goebbels was engaged in a Gandhian form of nonviolent resistance. And what Gandhi said he was committed to was not the absence of violence but **ahimsa**, which translated means negatively, nonviolence, and positively, the practice of love.[22] As John Yoder has suggested, in relation to the use of power, "To argue that 'the problem of power is all of one piece' is possible logically, but it gives the common abstraction 'power' priority over more significant variables. It is something like saying it is inconsistent for humans to practice contraception if they don't keep their dandelions from breeding, since 'the problem of sexual reproduction is all of a piece.'"[23] (Yoder, 1976: 41)

I am well aware of the difficulty of precision regarding all of the terms Niebuhr uses. However, it must be kept in mind that Niebuhr's broad way of using them biases the discussion in favor of the common abstractions rather than what might be argued are significant variables and differences.

For purposes of consistency I would suggest something like the following. My dictionary (*The American Heritage Dictionary*) defines power as "...the ability or capacity to act or perform effectively." And it defines force as the "...capacity to do work or cause physical change." I would suggest that both of those definitions are neutral (as regards the violence/nonviolence debate) and the words should probably be used as neutral words, unless a specific context makes it clear why the words have become negative.

Coerce is said by my dictionary to mean "...to dominate, to restrain, or control in a forcible way." Here we have moved into less neutral territory. However, we still need to be more careful than Niebuhr often is. I would argue there is a vast difference between my telling my son to go to bed (even forcefully if necessary) and my holding his hand to a hot stove or my dropping bombs on Dresdan. It is possible to use the same word to describe all three actions. But one has not helped in serious moral deliberation when one does so.

I would argue that it would be helpful to let violence be the word that names the phenomenon over which pacifists and non-pacifists disagree. However, even if this linguistic move would help, it still does not resolve what are real differences of opinion. But, at least it might help move people toward greater understanding of what those differences are. Violence according to my dictionary is "physical force exerted for the purpose of violating, damaging, or abusing." John Yoder argues that "...the core meaning of 'violence' resides in the dignity of the one offended."[24] Therefore, we might say that the core definition of violence is to violate a person's dignity.

As I said above, this effort at clarifying definitions does not resolve all differences of opinions either among pacifists, among non-pacifists, or between pacifists and non-pacifists. We, of course might debate what constitutes violation of a person's dignity. We might also debate at what point certain forms of coercion become violence.

What seems clear to me is that lethal violence quite clearly violates the dignity of the one killed. This is not to suggest that other acts short of killing might not also violate a person's dignity. In fact, there would be a few other acts, such as torture, that most everyone could agree also clearly are violence by this definition. However, many other acts would be much more ambiguous.

Is the drawing of some lines of demarcation, such as killing and torture, artificial? I think not. Again the analogy of marriage may help. In the marriage covenant, as normally understood, there are many acts that can potentially violate the covenant. There are few that can be indicated ahead of time as being clearly oft hat nature. Adultery is one. Having sexual intercourse with another person would clearly violate the covenant. That does not mean that other acts short of intercourse or of a different nature entirely might not violate the covenant. They might. But this act, by its very nature, violates the covenant. (However, since this violation does not terminate the life of either party involved there is still some hope of salvaging the covenant.) Similarly I would argue that lethal violence is clearly a line of demarcation regarding the violation of a person's dignity.

Next we turn to a discussion of Niebuhr's use of the terms necessity, impossibility, and responsibility. First, necessity. Niebuhr says that anyone who is involved in history will, by definition, be involved in the "...hard and cruel necessities of history...." which include the employment of violent coercion.[25] Again, Niebuhr has defined things in such a way that there appear to be no choices. As James Childress has put it, "The language of necessity implies that the society has no choice and that some action, such as war, is thus justifies or at least excused. But Niebuhr surely obfuscated matters by employing the language of necessity, which conceals specific value choices."[26] Necessity is an instrumental value not an absolute one. As John Yoder has put it, "Nothing is necessary in itself as far as ethics is concerned: an ant is necessary in view of a certain end."[27] That is, it is not necessary to eat unless one wants to avoid hunger. It is not necessary to support the "contras" in Nicaragua unless one has certain goals one believes they can help obtain. And those goals are justified according to some values one holds. To use necessity language in such situations simply papers over some significant moral issues.

Next I would like to make a few comments about Niebuhr's use of the term "impossibility" specifically as it relates to the impossibility of embodying selfless love in history.[28] Again Niebuhr has used a word with a multiplicity of meanings to obfuscate the real issues.[29] If by impossibility Niebuhr means that humanity and society are metaphysically corrupted by sin, he certainly would not therefore conclude that significant moral choices are rendered meaningless? And just because there are no perfectly loving moral agents does not mean that there can be no moral acts that are sufficiently reflective of the sacrificial, selfless love of Jesus that they are not recognizable as such. Some would argue that within supportive Christian communities such acts can be sustained relatively consistently over a significant period of time.

There are a number of other reasons why selfless, loving, nonviolent acts might be thought "impossible." Distinguishing the different meanings helps further ethical deliberation about the issues involved. Nonviolence might be deemed impossible because love is not considered binding or some other value is deemed more important. Nonviolence might be "impossible" because an individual or group is unwilling to pay the cost entailed by the loving, nonviolent deeds. Nonviolence may be "impossible" because the moral agent(s) have insufficient information, creativity, or material resources to accomplish desired goals. Nonviolence may be "impossible" because the moral agent(s) are acting in a situation over which they have little or no control. Nonviolence may be "impossible" because the moral agent(s) are acting in a situation over which they have little or no control. Nonviolence may be "impossible" because the moral agent(s) misjudged. After carrying out a series of acts thought to be consistent with loving nonviolence, it was realized there were unintended violent consequences. These different reasons for the "impossibility" of nonviolence matter significantly in moral deliberations.

Finally a few comments about another complicated concept, responsibility. Niebuhr said that, "A responsible relationship to the political order...makes an unqualified disavowal of violence impossible."[30] Furthermore, he said that "...nonviolence may be covert violence. Children do starve and old people freeze to death in the poverty of our cities, a poverty for which everyone who has more than the bare necessities of life must feel some responsibility."[31] There is no question but that it is good for us who are comfortable to be reminded of the suffering of many people in the world. And it is good for us to be reminded that we should be as responsible as we can in doing our part in alleviating that suffering. However, I'm not sure in what sense I am really morally culpable for the death of a child in Harlem due to starvation. And that for reasons related to geography, physical limitations, social structures, actual causes of this particular child's starvation, etc. And what I am willing and unwilling to do to make things happen according to my responsibility is, again, rooted in values and commitments. As John Yoder has said: "Of course, according to pacifist belief, there exists a real Christian responsibility for the social order, but that responsibility is a derivative of Christian love, not a contradictory and self-defining ethical norm."[32]

PACIFISM AND POLITICS

Finally, I would like to sketch very briefly the general outline of one way to think about A Christian pacifist's relation to social and political realities. First, Christian ethics are for Christians. The commitment to follow Jesus in the way of the cross is binding only on those who confess Jesus as Lord. That means that the pacifist doesn't assume a pacifist commitment on the part of others who don't make such a confession (or on the part of those who do not believe the confession entails loving enemies in tangible ways). And it certainly means that the pacifist doesn't apply a pacifist ethic directly to social and political structures.

However, on the other hand a pacifist does not have to assume that no one outside the Church will be open to or even committed to values, even nonviolence, with which the pacifist would be comfortable. But the Christological pacifist would realize that the others probably have something of a different framework for their values, a framework that might make a significant difference at certain points.

Being committed to nonviolence also does not mean that a pacifist need ignore the sometimes significant moral differences among nation states and other social structures as those relate to the use of violence--overt and covert. Being committed to nonviolence does not, in other words, cancel one's ability to distinguish lesser and greater forms of violence and injustice. For a Christological pacifist the standard for justice is Jesus (in the context of the whole canon of Scripture). This is somewhat similar to Niebuhr' use of love as a discriminating principle. However, I would argue that there is more substance to this Jesus and he functions within this framework more substantively for moral guidance.[33]

To repeat what was said above, because of the reality of the fallenness of the world, the state (or other social structures in the world) would not be addressed as if they could have or do have any commitment to reflect the standard of Jesus. Rather the state would be addressed about specific violent or unjust abuses that it would be reasonable for the state to correct. In fact, often states make claims about their standards of justice. Therefore, often it is the states' own claims to which appeal can be made.

I also want to mention briefly the need to take even more seriously than Niebuhr did the possibilities of nonviolent direct action movements. Gandhi and King have shown us what sweeping changes can be wrought through such movements. Social scientists such as Gene Sharp have shown how such strategies can have even wider applications and effectiveness. And some who embrace the sort of Christological pacifism I'm referring to have given serious attention to these issues.[34]

Thus far I have spoken about ways to think about pacifists addressing themselves to the political structures but I have not addressed myself to the issue of their actual involvement in politics. This is often one of the first questions people address to pacifists. They ask some variation of, "But how could you run a country with pacifism?" There are various reasons why that is not one of the first questions that should be addressed to the pacifism to which I am referring.[35]

Aside from all of the other reasons, it is a simple fact that most of us are not going to be generals or presidents but rather lowly privates or voters who are represented by people who truly claim to represent us. "We" are not the government as it is sometimes thought. That is mythology. A few powerful, rich people in Washington (and global corporations) run our nation state. But let me just say that Christological pacifists are not automatically excluded from most positions. The Quakers ran Pennsylvania for almost seventy years. Only a few years ago Harold Hughes served as, first, governor and, then, Senator from Idaho while being a pacifist.

CONCLUSION

My conclusion is really quite brief. I believe Niebuhr established an artificial dilemma. There is no reason why a Christian has to choose between a commitment to nonviolence and serious concern for and involvement in the world. It does mean, of course that certain means will not be used no matter what the end. But for anyone committed to any moral values that is true. For instance, someone within the just war tradition might not intentionally target civilians even if that act might win a battle, a war, or save thousands of lives. The alternative to such an approach is a kind of consequentialism that simply throws moral principles regarding means out the window.

It also means that within our world of global awareness all of us, including pacifists, must express tangible concern for the suffering of the multitudes. It means that pacifists who care about justice must be attentive to the methods of the Gandhis and Kings of the world. And North American middle class pacifists, as well as everyone else who lives a comfortable existence, should be understanding of people in violent and grossly unjust circumstances who lash out in retaliation. Let us all pray and work for a just and peaceful world.

ENDNOTES

1. James F. Childress, "Reinhold Niebuhr's Realistic Critique of Pacifism," *Moral Responsibility in Conflicts: Essays on Nonviolence, War, and Conscience,* James F. Childress (Baton Rouge, LA: Louisiana State University Press, p. 37.

2. Reinhold Niebuhr, *Reinhold Niebuhr on Politics: His Political Philosophy and Its Application to Our Age As Expressed in His Writings,* ed. Harry R. Davis and Robert C. Good (NY: Charles Scribner's Sons, 1960), 149. (Davis & Good)

3. Davis & Good, p. 150.

4. John H. Yoder, *Christian Attitudes to War, Peace, and Revolution: A Companion to Bainton* (Elkhart, IN: Co-lp Bookstore, 1983), p. 356.

5. Charles W. Kegley, ed., *Reinhold Niebuhr: His Religious, Social, and Political Thought* (NY: The Pilgrim Press, 1984), pp. 73. 118.

6. See, e.g.: John H. Yoder, *Nevertheless,* Rev. ed., (Scottdale, PA: Herald Press, 1976); Yoder, *Christian Attitudes.*

7. John H. Yoder, *Nevertheless,* pp. 123-128.

8. Reinhold Niebuhr, *Christianity and Power Politics* (NY: Charles Scribner's Sons, 1940), pp. 8-9.

9. Reinhold Niebuhr, *Leaves from the Notebooks of a Tamed Cynic* (NY: Meridian Books, 1957), p. 30.

10. Niebuhr, *Christianity and Power Politics,* p. 10.

11. Richard J. Cassidy, *Jesus, Politics, and Society: A Study of Luke's Gospel* (Maryknoll, NY: Orbis Books, 1978).

12. Marcus J. Borg, *Conflict, Holiness & Politics in the Teachings of Jesus* (NY: The Edwin Mellen Press, 1984); cf.: Richard A. Horsley, *Jesus and the Spiral of Violence* (NY: Harper & Row, 1987).

13. Reinhold Niebuhr, *The Nature and Destiny of Man, Vol. II: Human Nature* (NY: Charles Scribner's Sons), pp. 107-126.

14. See, e.g.: John H. Yoder, *The Politics of Jesus* (Grand Rapids, Mich.: Wm. B. Eerdmans, 1972), pp. 94-232; Krister Stendahl, *Paul Among Jews and Gentiles* (Philadelphia: Fortress Press, 1976); Stephen Westerholm, *Israel's Law and the Church's Faith* (Grand Rapids, Mich.: Wm. B. Eerdmans, 1988).

15. John H. Yoder, "How 'Absolutes' Are Qualified," Unpublished memorandum for "whom it may concern," August 12, 1985, 5pp.

16. Yoder, "How 'Absolutes' Are Qualified," p. 3.

17. Stanley Hauerwas, *The Peaceable Kingdom: A Primer in Christian Ethics* (Notre Dame, IN: University of Notre Dame Press, p. 30.

18. Kegley, p. 13.

19. Hauerwas, p. 94.

20. Hauerwas, pp. 96ff.; John H. Yoder, *The Original Revolution,* Rev. ed. (Scottdale, PA: Herald Press, 1977), pp. 107ff.

21. Davis & Good, p. 140.

22. Mohandas Gandhi, *All Men Are Brothers: Life and Thoughts of Mahatma Gandhi As Told In His Own Words,* ed. Krishna Kripalani (Chicago: World Without War Publications, 1958), pp. 77-97.

23. John H. Yoder, *Nevertheless,* p. 41.

24. John H. Yoder, "Fuller Definition of 'Violence'," Unpublished memorandum prepared for a World Council of Churches study group, March 28, 1973, 7pp.; see also: Robert McAfee Brown, *Religion and Violence* (Philadelphia: The Westminster Press, 1973), p. 7.

25. Reinhold Niebuhr, *Love and Justice: Selections from the Shorter Writings of Reinhold Niebuhr,* ed. D. B. Robertson (Gloucester, Mass.: Peter Smith, 1976), p. 223. (Robertson)

26. Childress, p. 45.

27. John H. Yoder, "Reinhold Niebuhr and Christian Pacifism," *The Mennonite Quarterly Review,* 29 (April, 1955), 113.

28. See, e.g.: Reinhold Niebuhr, *An Interpretation of Christian Ethics* (NY: Meridian Books, 1958), 97ff.

29. For the discussion of impossibility that follows I am indebted to: Yoder, "Reinhold Niebuhr and Christian Pacifism," pp. 107-108, 112-113.

30. Niebuhr, *An Interpretation,* p. 170.

31. Robertson, p. 257.

32. Yoder, "Reinhold Niebuhr and Christian Pacifism," p. 113.

33. See, e.g.: John H. Yoder, *The Christian Witness to the State,* 3rd ed. (Newton, KS: Faith and Life Press, 1977).

34. See, e.g.: Duane K. Friesen, *Christian Peacemaking & International Conflict: A Realist Pacifist Perspective* (Scottdale, PA: Herald Press, 1986).

35. John H. Yoder, *The Priestly Kingdom* (Notre Dame, IN: University of Notre Dame Press, 1984), pp. 135-147.

CHAPTER FOUR

A PREFERENCE FOR SENECA OVER CICERO:
Attitudes of the Brethren of the Common Life
to Classical Literature

Wade F. Bradshaw
Trinity Evangelical Divinity School

The historiography of the Brethren of the Common Life makes the graceful sweep of a bell-shaped curve so beloved a the symbol of balance and symmetry to the physical sciences. Almost completely ignored even in the Low Countries until the Twentieth Century, they grew in perceived importance until in the works of Dutch-born and American-trained Albert Hyma they reached a dizzying zenith as a movement of "world-historical significance."[1] The works of Spoelhoff[2] and Henkel,[3] both students of Hyma, begin to look into the subject in greater detail and finally we come to the efforts of R. R. Post, Emeritus Professor of Medieval History in the University of Nijmegen. His careful reexamination of the interpretations and somewhat daring assumptions of his predecessors brings on the flattening out of the curve. To the student who has come under the spell of this attractive movement of Christian reform, the words of Professor Post come as a needed blast of reality after the heady conjectures of Hyma, "Not everything that was devout in the late Middle Ages formed part of the Modern Devotion."[4]

The terminology is not helpful. The Brethren were a lay movement and, rejecting formal vows, were by definition an organism of hazy boundaries. Much of the disagreement between Hyma and Post stems from their including or rejecting several significant individuals as members of the Brethren. Even worse is the ubiquitous term *Devotio Moderna* which can be seen, by those who choose to, behind every increment of progress or any increase in lay piety from the middle of the Quattrocento until the Act of Supremacy of Henry VIII.[5]

Hyma made an unfortunate attempt to clear these waters with his usage of "Christian Renaissance", explaining that to use the term 'Devotio moderna' frequently, makes one's book difficult to read, while the English equivalent 'New Devotion' is lacking in color and effect.[6]

This solution evidences the high regard that the author places on the movement, and perhaps it is more pleasing to read; but surely it is both too grandiose and too quick to label by implication the Renaissance in the South as pagan at best, if not actually anti-Christian. But if Hyma's admiration causes him to reach too high, the arc must not be allowed to drop forever, until the Brethren are yet once more neglected in the shadows between the art of the Italians and the theology of the Germans.

For the Brethren of the Common Life did make, by all scholars' conclusions, some outstanding contributions. They were at least partially responsible for the education of Hegius, Thomas a Kempis, Agricola, Erasmus, Wessel Gansfort and Adrian VI; even Luther himself spent a year absorbing their spirit and tuition at Magdeburg. This is accomplishment enough, without need to make tenuous speculations as to their influence upon John Sturm's schools in Germany and Colet's at ST. Paul's in London.[7] Nevertheless, the success of the schools in Deventer and Zwolle, Munster and Utrecht (among numerous others) speaks praise enough for the innovations in discipline, organization and curriculum begun by the likes of Cele, Hegius, Murmellius and Dringenberg. The Devotio Moderna did effect reform amongst the monasticism of the period. And beyond doubt, even if its author's identity may not be, is the contribution of the movement to a lasting devotional literature that transcends the fences between Catholicism and Protestantism in the form of the *De Imitatione Christi*, routinely touted as the most read book upon the coattails of the Scriptures themselves, and putting Loyola's *Spiritual Exercises* in its debt.

These contributions, notwithstanding the internecine debate as to their particulars and their extent, must win a lasting place of honor for the self-effacing Brethren. A contumacious problem remains in the relationship between the *Devotio Moderna* and the rise of the Northern Humanism. Oh, there are links that upon superficial examination appear to join the two by iron: Erasmus did indeed study with the Brothers for eleven years at Deventer and learned his Greek there rather than at Oxford; and yes, Alexander Hegius taught the elements of Hebrew when such knowledge was rare north of the Alps. Post takes a critical look and finds some of the links remain of suspect strength,

> Every writer who examines the history of the origin, progress
> and nature of Humanism, is compelled to tackle this
> problem and usually concludes, or at least asserts, that the
> Devotio Moderna and the Brethren of the Common Life,
> fostered the rise of Humanism.[8]

If the Brethren can be shown to play so critical a role in the emergence of the
new learning and love of the ancients that is Humanism, then, Christian or
not, we must allow Hyma's "Renaissance" to stand. If the relationship be so
intimate, then we ought to expect to find in the features of the parent at least
a general resemblance to those obvious in the child.

One such feature of Humanism seen in both its northern and southern
expressions is a remarkable admiration for the old, and embarrassingly pagan,
classics. If the Brethren spawned the authors of *Enchiridion* and *Invectiva,*
then we may look to them for just such an admiration of the Greeks and
Romans.

The search begins with Geert Groote, who almost all agree is the Source of
the Brothers and Sisters of the Common Life and the Augustinian Canons
Regular of the Windesheim Congregation. These are the three movements
which bound the much more elusive "Devotio Moderna."

His driving passion was to see reform in a Church which suffered under the
"Babylonian Captivity" of Avignon and was himself an Urbanist in the Great
Schism. His religious conversion occurred in 1374, leaving him only ten active
years in which to effect all of his wide-reaching influence. The weight of that
influence is all the more astounding when one realizes that his vocation as an
itinerant preacher in the Yssel valley was brought to an end after only four
years when in 1383 a clergy predictably stung to jealousy by Groote's "Sermon
Against the Immoral Clergy" convinced the Bishop of Utrecht to ban the
deacon, who felt him self unworthy of ordination, from publicly preaching.

Groote spent thirteen years studying at the University of Paris and acquiring
a respectable command of the Canon Law and the *Corpus Juris Civilis.* Most
accounts of his life refer to his voracious appetite for books, one so great that
he hauled about great boxes of them with him to use in his sermons. At
times he had as many as five copyists working on manuscripts for him, and
just prior to his death he arranged for a committee of three of the Brothers
known as "the Guardians of Groote's Books" to insure the safe maintenance
of his accumulated library.[9] Among those authorities and authors to which
he alluded are:

the Bible, Albert Magnus, Ambrose, Anselm, Antony, Apuleius, Aristotle, Augustine [especially], Bede, Bernard of Clairvaux [again especially], Boethius Bonaventura, Cassianus, Cato, Chrysostom, Cicero, Climacus, Cyprian, Demosthenes, Dionysius, Eusebius, Fabricius, Francis of Assisi, Gregory, Gregory of Nianza, Henry of Ghent, Hippocrates, Isidor, Jerome, Juvenal, Lucan, Lyra, Nepos, Permenianus Donatista, Peter of Damiani, Plato, Pliny, Seneca, Socrates, Suetonius, Suso, Theophrastus, Aquinas, Valerius, Vegetius, Virgil and the Canon Law.[10]

This list shows an admirable depth and breadth of reading - there are classical names included in it; but really it is not unusual for a medieval scholar of any stature.[11]   Certainly it would not have been the envy of a   Boccaccio or Salutati.

Groote's undeniable interest in education was more pragmatic than pure and disinterested. He is out to reform the Church, and what better way than to educate young men who may then go on to university and into the clergy? He shared with Wycliffe an interest both in preaching and a Bible in the vernacular.[12] But it was the saving of souls that occupied for him the position of *ars artium*.[13] His own letters and collected sayings reveal Groote as a reformer, a bitter critic of scholasticism, a proponent of the *via antiqua* and suspicious of education for its own sake:

Spend no time at geometry, arithmetic, rhetoric, dialectic, grammar, lyric poetry, civil law, or astrology. For Seneca already reproached all these things as something the good man should look on with a wary eye: how much more ought they to be repudiated by the spiritual man and the Christian![14]

or again:

Among all the pagan disciplines moral philosophy is the least reprehensible, often very useful and beneficial for both your own self and for teaching others. The wiser men such as Socrates and Plato, accordingly reduced all philosophy to ethics. . . . Seneca therefore, following this, liberally included ethical matters in his *Natural Questions*. For whatever does not make us better or restrain us from evil is harmful.

This is Groote's philosophy of education encapsulated. He warns of its dangers while at the same instant exhibiting his own familiarity with the material almost in spite of himself. But all learning is to be measured by its usefulness in bringing its recipient virtue; he is not an obscurantist, still this falls short of what is usually considered the Humanist attitude.

Groote's ideas and opinions launched the three-pronged movement of the *Devotio Moderna*, but what of those Brethren who followed him? Was it these who diverged from their master's warnings and attitudes towards secular learning?

When John Cele, rector of the school at Zwolle (1375-1417), decided to retire into a monastery, it was his best friend Groote who prevailed upon him to stay at his work among the schoolboys sent to him rather than to schools in even much larger cities. Here we clearly see our problem in identification; Post will not consider Cele as formally part of the Brethren, while Hyma sees any of his many accomplishments to be immediately counted in favor of the *Devotio Moderna*. Cele's reforms in school hours, loving discipline and division of students into eight grades now seem common sensical; but in his day they were dramatic, and they reaped tremendous results. He was "the first important teacher to introduce the study of the Bible into the elementary schools,"[16] and his methods

> sought to inculcate a love for individual research by letting
> pupils delve among the classics rather than confine them-
> selves to text-books, and taught the boys the vernacular as
> well.[17]

This is just the sort of atmosphere that one would expect to find behind a product such as a Desiderus Erasmus, who was in fact a student under Cele. In his *De Ratione Studii* Erasmus set forth his opinions for school reform: Greek literature was to be taught along with Latin; there was not to be too much grammar; the children were to read the sources for themselves; and scholastic works were to be replaced by the Bible itself.[18]

> Whereas many leaders of the Italian Renaissance studied the
> classics for style only, the men of Deventer, Zwolle, Schletts-
> tadt, and Munster delved into the mine and found fine
> phrases, but greater treasures in wisdom.[19]

This is Groote all over again, and it is the attitude seen in Erasmus' preference of Seneca over Cicero "because the Brethren of the Common Life had learned from Groote to value practical advice on moral questions above mere rhetoric."[20] Erasmus never acknowledged such an indebtedness, and we are not, therefore, able to state the case too forcefully. Nevertheless, Hyma's circumstantial evidence in this instance seems compelling.

Alexander Hegius was Cele's truest successor. He taught at Emmerich from 1475-1483 and then at St. Lebwin's in Deventer until his death in 1498. Hyma considers him the greatest teacher in Transalpine Europe in the fifteenth century;[21] Post believes his appointment to Emmerich a sign of the Brother's plan to renew education in the Humanistic spirit.[22]   In Hegius we have progressed beyond Groote's more medieval attitudes, and this may be symptomatic of the century that separated the two. Hegius learned his Greek from the unabashedly Humanistic Agricola; in his teaching he set aside certain time-honored medieval texts and in his *Farrago* suggested in their stead a return tot he clear diction of Cicero, Virgil, and Sallust and an honest imitation of the Italian Humanists.[23] Again in Hegius, however, we see in the Northern Renaissance a genius for taking the same interests as those pursued in the South and bending them for moral and religious purposes. Those in the tradition of the Brethren of the Common Life exhibit an apt restraint that makes them appear less modern to our eyes than their Italian contemporaries. A portrait by Butzbach, one of Hegius' students, reveals him as a teacher but yet still very much involved in the relief of the poor and sick, a practice which Hyma maintains makes him very different from the Southern Humanists.[24]

When we come to Rudolf Agricola (1442-1485), as already mentioned, we deal with one about whom there is no doubt as to his attitude toward classical literature.   Both Post and Hyma approve of his credentials as a true Humanist; both concur as to his pedigree in the *Devotio Moderna* as well. This "Petrarch of Germany" according to Spitz, "stood with roots deep in the piety of the Brethren of the Common Life."[25] Like so many other notable characters, he passed through that remarkable school at Deventer; but he went on to study at Louvain and Italy (Rome and Ferrara).[26] The problem for scholars is deciding how much influence to apportion to which period of education. If he returned to Germany in 1480 after many years abroad, is not his love of Greek and Latin authors just as likely to be due to his exposure to the ferment of fifteenth century Italy as to his "roots" amid the burgeoning capitalism of the Yssel valley?

One tires after a while of reading the various historians claiming the best-known names to decorate their varying theories and begins to despair the existence of any "hard" evidence. Hyma tries to rectify this situation with a very interesting survey of incunabula in *The Christian Renaissance*. At last it appears that we are being presented with lists and figures that cannot but speak honestly for themselves. Much of this same material is rehearsed again in Strand's *The Brethren of the Common Life and Fifteenth Century Printing.*[27]

The Brothers and Sisters of the Common Life had from their very beginnings been busy in the copying of manuscripts. Groote had believed strongly in the dignity of manual labor and had forbidden his followers to beg. The use of movable-type can, therefore, be seen as radically effecting the movement. but one is more than once struck by the resourcefulness of the Brethren, and within a decade of Gutenberg they were busy operating presses of their own. They operated the first presses at Brussels and Gouda (in Southern Holland) as well as Marenthal, Rostock and Lübeck.

Deventer, the original home of Groote, exceeded every other city in the Low Countries with its astounding production of 500-600 editions, and Zwolle produced 100 of its own--a very respectable number. The figures do not, however, bear their proper weight until highlighted against those from other areas. The grand total of incunabula for all of England was 364. That is, England's output was twenty percent that of the Low Countries' and only about 2/5 of that of the city of Deventer alone.[28] Sheer numbers, however, do not advance our cause by much; we are interested in gaining a sense of ancient and classical texts produced. Strand informs us that the Brothers,

> were not only exceptionally eager to disseminate knowledge,
> but they also frequently struck a rather uncommon median
> by revealing interest in both theological works and the
> classics and by using both Latin and the vernacular.[29]

and again,

> The type of book printed and not just the number is also
> interesting. The majority are religious and of a practical
> religious nature, but a remarkably large percentage repre-
> sented classical works.[30]

Of the 508 editions listed by Hyma for Deventer ninety of these are classical works (Greek or Latin).[31] Not only does this ratio show a greater interest in classics by Deventer than other areas, but as Strand calculates, "The number of classical books printed in Paris is probably smaller than that for the little town of Deventer."[32]

Here at last it seems is proof positive of a commitment by the *Devotio Moderna* to classical literature. The picture, however, changes somewhat when the presses operated by the Brothers themselves are studied separately rather than grouped with those in the area about them. They clearly remain interested in printing; they are publishing classical works such as Ovid's *Fasti* and *Metamorphoses;* but if one is pushed to admit that the tremendous explosion of printing in Deventer cannot irrefutably be shown to be solely under the influence of the Brothers, then one likewise must conclude, rather anticlimactically, with Mr. Strand that how important were the effects of the Brothers of the Common Life upon fifteenth-century printing will probably never be clearly answered.[33]

Our hard evidence has proven as malleable and ambivalent as tracing the lives of individual scholars or listening to the voices of more recent ones. A vague impression is left that if Hyma was not correct in his estimation of just how important the *Devotio Moderna* was, that his attitude of respect was not misplaced and may even have something to commend itself over the more critical scholarship of Post. We must agree with Professor Jacob that "we should be in error if we attributed to them the character of Renaissance humanists."[34] The primary interest of the Brothers of the Common Life, even in the midst of their many educational efforts, was not academic. Perhaps our vague impression should not surprise us. Gerard Groote and his followers after all disapproved of studies being undertaken for prestige or worldly gain. *The Imitation of Christ,* by far the most fruitful and far-reaching of the movement's creations warns:

> Truly at the day of judgement we shall not be examined on
> what we have read, but on what we have don; not how well
> we have said, but how religiously we have lived.[35]

ENDNOTES

1. Regerus Richardus Post, *The Modern Devotion,* in Studies in Medieval and Reformation Thought, vol. 3 (Leiden: E. J. Brill, 1968).

2. William Spoelhoff, Concepts of religious nonconformity and religious toleration as developed by the Brethren of the Common Life in the Netherlands, 1374-1489. Unpublished doctoral thesis, University of Michigan, 1946.

3. Julia S. Henkel, *A Historical Study of the Educational Contributions of the Brethren of the Common Life,* 1962 PhD. University of Pittsburg.

4. Post, *The Modern Devotion,* p. 4.

5. A. G. Dickens, *The English Reformation* (New York: Schocken Books, 1964), p. 14. Dickens himself argues against inflating the role of the New Devotion's influence upon the Lollards of England.

6. Albert Hyma, *The Christian Renaissance & a History of the "Devotio Moderna"* (Hamden, Connecticut: Anchor Books, 1965), p. 518.

7. Julia S. Henkel, *School Organizational Patterns of the Brethren of the Common Life* p. 331, 334 in The Dawn of Modern Civilization ed. Kenneth A. Strand (Ann Arbor: Ann Arbor Publishers, 1962). This is a collection of festschriften for Albert Hyma. Her suggested linkages between the Brothers and Sturm and Colet, while not unbelievable, seem far from certain.

8. Post, *The Modern Devotion,* p. 1.

9. Albert Hyma, *The Brethren of the Common Life* (Grand Rapids: Eerdmans, 1950) p. 45.

10. Ibid., p. 26.

11. Post, *The Modern Devotion,* p. 84.

12. The two men were contemporaries and died in the same year, 1384.

13. Post, *The Modern Devotion,* p. 110.

14. John van Engen, ed., *The Devotio Moderna: Basic Writings in the Classics of Western Spirituality.* (New York: Paulist Press, 1981) p. 67.

15. Ibid., p. 67.

16. Hyma, *The Brethren of the Common Life,* p. 11.

17. Ibid., p. 163.

18. Hyma, *The Christian Renaissance,* p. 295.

19. Hyma, *The Brethren of the Common Life,* p. 124.

20. Hyma, *The Christian Renaissance,* p. 229.

21. Hyma, *The Brethren of the Common Life,* p. 119.

22. Post, *The Modern Devotion,* p. 421.

23. Hyma, *The Brethren of the Common Life,* p. 119.

24. Ibid., p. 121, from the *Auctarium* by Butzbach, p. 238.

25. Lewis W. Spitz, *The Religious Renaissance of the German Humanists* (Cambridge, Mass: Harvard University Press, 1963) p. 39.

26. Henry S. Lucas, *The Renaissance and the Reformation* (New York: Harper and Brothers Publishers, 1934) p. 372.

27. Kenneth A. Strand, "The Brethren of the Common Life and Fifteenth-Century Printing," in *The Dawn of Modern Civilization,* ed. Strand, 1970.

28. Ibid., p. 345.

29. Ibid., p. 343.

30. Ibid., p. 345.

31. Hyma, *The Christian Renaissance,* p. 608.

32. Strand, p. 345.

33. Ibid., p. 350.

34. E. F. Jacob, *Gerard Groote and the Beginnings of the New Devotion in the Low Countries,* Journal of Ecclesiastical History, vol. 3 1952 p. 56.

35. Thomas à Kempis, *The Imitation of Christ,* trans. Richard Whitford, ed. by Edward J. Klein (New York: Harper & Brothers Publishers, 1941) p. 9.

BIBLIOGRAPHY

General Bibliographies of the *'Devotio moderna':*

Alberts, W. Jappe.   *Zur Historiografie der Devotio Moderna und ihrer Erforschung,* vol. 11. West falische: Forschungen, 1953. 51-67.

Dols, Jean Michel Emile. *Bibliographie der Moderne devotie, bibliotheekte Nijmegen.* II Nijmegen: N. V. Centrale drukkerif, 1936.

Other Works:

Aston, Margaret E. "The Northern Renaissance." In *The Meaning of the Renaissance,* ed. R. DeMolen, 71-129. Boston: Houghton Miffin, 1974.

Henkel, Julia S. "An Historical Study of the Educational Contributions of the Brethren of the Common Life." Ph.D. diss., University of Pittsburg, 1962.

Henkel, Julia S. "Geert Groote." In *A History of Religious Educators,* ed. Elmer L. Towns, 82-91. Grand Rapids: Baker Book House, 1975.

Henkel, Julia S. "School Organizational Patterns of the Brethren of the Common Life." In *The Dawn of Modern Studies,* ed. K. A. Strand, 323-338. Ann Arbor: Ann Arbor Publishers, 1962.

Hyma, Albert. *Renaissance to Reformation.* Grand Rapids: Eerdmans, 1955.

Hyma, Albert. *The Christian Renaissance: A History of the "Devotio Moderna".* Hamden, Connecticut: Anchor Books, 1965.

Hyma, Albert. *The Youth of Erasmus.* Ann Arbor: University of Michigan Press, 1930.

Jacob, Ernest F. "Gerard Groote and the Beginnings of the New Devotion in the Low Countries." *Journal of Ecclesiastical History 3* (January-April 1952). 40-57.

à Kempis, Thomas. *The Imitation of Christ.* Translated by Edward J. Klein. New York, London: Harper & Row Publishers, 1941.

McShane, Edward J. "The History of the Church from 1300 to 1648: A Survey of Research, 1955-1960." *Theological Studies 22* (1961). 59-85.

Mulder, Willelmus S. J., ed. *Gerardi Magni Epistolae.* Tielt: Lannoo, 1933.

Post, Regerus Richardus. *The Modern Devotion.* Leiden: Brill, 1968.

Spitz, Lewis W.   *The Religious Renaissance of the German Humanists.* Cambridge, Mass: Harvard University Press, 1963.

Spoelhof, William.   "Concepts of Religious Nonconformity and Religious Toleration as Developed by the Brethren of the Common Life in the Netherlands." Ph.D. diss., University of Michigan, 1946.

Strand, Kenneth A.   "The Brethren of the Common Life: A Review Article of R. R. Post's *The Modern Devotion.*" Andrews University Semitic Studies 8:1 (1970). 65-76.

van Engen, John, trans. "Devotio Moderna: Basic Writings." In *The Classics of Western Spirituality.* New York: Paulist Press, 1968.

CHAPTER FIVE

THE FAMILY AS DOMESTIC CHURCH

Gregory J. Konerman
Mt. St. Mary's Seminary of the West

ABSTRACT

A theological understanding of the family as "domestic Church" is examined. Understood as living sacrament, the Christian family is seen as having a radical call to manifest the threefold mission of Christ. This implies very serious considerations for discernment of the vocation of marriage.

INTRODUCTION

One extremely significant, though seemingly under-emphasized, feature of the doctrines of Vatican Council II is its teachings on the nature and mission of the Christian family. Those Catholics who are either formally engaged to be married, or are in some process of discernment about a decision to marry, should take special heed of what the Church is teaching about the way of life which they are contemplating. For indeed, it is a very radical message, and one which has little in common with many of the humanistic conceptualizations about marriage and the family which are prevalent in our modern Western society.

REVIEW OF CHURCH TEACHING

Certainly the Church's attention to the family is nothing new. We have evidence of the importance of family life in the early Church in various accounts in *The Acts of the Apostles* and in the *Epistles of Paul,* wherein we are told of the "household Churches" of the apostolic era and also of family conversions. We also find references to the importance of the family in the writings of the early Church Fathers, such as Augustine who speaks of the significance of family prayer and family catechesis, as well as John Chrysostom who praised family gatherings as "true ekklesia."

MARRIAGE AND FAMILY AS DOMESTIC CHURCH

The more recent teachings on the Christian family, however, can best be understood in the context of the doctrines of the laity which are so central to the message of Vatican Council II. Certainly one of the most important promulgations of Vatican Council II is the teaching that **all** baptized Christians are equally called to holiness, that each baptized person is called to be a full disciple of Jesus Christ. As stated in *Lumen Gentium:*

> "...all are called to sanctity, and have obtained an equal privilege of faith through the justice of God" (Lg. 32) and furthermore, "...the Faithful, who by Baptism are incorporated into Christ, are placed in the People of God, and in their own way share the priestly, prophetic, and kingly office of Christ, and to the best of their ability carry on the mission of the whole Christian people in the Church and in the world" (Lg. 31).

In light of this understanding that **all** are called "to the fullness of Christian life" (Lg. 40), the vocation of marriage and family life takes on greater dimension and importance. For just as each baptized person is called to holiness, so too then the family as "the first and vital cell of society" is seen as a sacred group or community which is called to holiness with the mission of being "domestic sanctuary of the Church" (*Decree on the Laity,* 11). The family, as constituted by the inter-relationships between its members, is called to be a kind of process of sanctification wherein each member assists every other toward holiness. The sacred Council explains to us in *Lumen Gentium* that:

> "...in virtue of the sacrament of Matrimony... Christian married couples help one another to attain holiness in their married life and in the rearing oft heir children... from the marriage of Christians there comes the family in which new citizens of human society are born and, by the grace of the Holy Spirit in Baptism, those are made children of God so that the People of God may be perpetuated throughout the centuries. In what might be regarded as the domestic

Church, the parents, by word and example, are the first
heralds of faith with regard to their children" (Lg. 11).

The Christian family, then, is described as constituting its own locus of
Church. The family of baptized Christians is defined as being a miniature or
small-scale Church. The family **is** Church. This is based upon the understanding that its members, by virtue of their intimate relationships with each
other "help each other to attain holiness", and as such they constitute a
sacramental entity which then "signifies and shares in" the divine love of
Christ. This is elaborated on in *Lumen Gentium,* as follows:

> "Christian married couples and parents, following their own
> way, should support one another in grace all through life
> with faithful love, and should train their children (lovingly
> received from God) in Christian doctrine and evangelical
> virtues. Because in this way they present to all an example
> of unfailing and generous love, they build up the brother-
> hood of charity, and they stand as witnesses and cooperators
> of the fruitfulness of Mother Church, as a sign of and a
> share in that love with which Christ loved his Bride and gave
> Himself for Her" (Lg. 41).

DOMESTIC CHURCH AS SACRAMENT: Sign and Instrument

Thus, there is a sacramental essence to marriage and the family. This
sacramental quality does not consist merely in the wedding ceremony or the
exchange of vows. It is rather that those initial public vows mark the
beginning of an on-going and progressing sacramental **relationship** which then
expands and incorporates the entire family. It is this life-long commitment to
relationship, and the development of that relationship, which are in essence
sacramental. As such, the relationship is both a **sign of** and an **instrument of**
God's grace.

The relationship is a sign of the Divine in that it is a reflection of the absolute
fidelity of God to His people and of the perfect love of God for His people.
In its faithfulness and on-going love, the marriage relationship is a symbol of
God's Revelation. As explained by the Council in *Gaudium et Spes:*

> "The Christian family springs from marriage, which is an
> image and a sharing in the partnership of love between
> Christ and the Church; it will show forth to all men Christ's

living presence in the world and the authentic nature of the
Church by the love and generous fruitfulness of the spouses,
by their unity and fidelity, and by the loving way in which all
members of the family cooperate with each other" (Gs. 48).

The relationship is an instrument for God's grace that makes the relating
possible, that sustains it, and that operates within it to enable ever-greater
growth and development. Just as in the Incarnation God brought Revelation
to its fullness and made possible an intimate personal relationship between
God and humankind, so too God's grace makes possible the intimate love and
devotedness in marital and family relationships. God's grace is operant in
these relationships, thus constituting the imperative (or instrumental) aspect
of sacrament. In *Gaudium et Spes* it is described as follows:

"Authentic married love is caught up into divine love and is
directed and enriched by the redemptive power of Christ and
the salvific action of the Church, with the result that the
spouses are effectively led to God and are helped and
strengthened in their lofty role as father and mother..." (Gs.
48).

In his *Apostolic Exhortation on the Family*, (*Familiaris Consortio*), delivered
in 1981, Pope John Paul II spoke about this sacramental essence of the
marital relationship. He explains that all humankind is called to form a
"communion of persons," according to the message as found in Genesis,--" to
increase, multiply and fill the earth, and subdue it." He then describes the
family as the first and most important communion (Fc. 19 & 21). He explains
to us that St. Paul's comparison of the marital union with the relationship of
Christ and His Church, (Eph. 5:25-31) is based upon the understanding that
both are communions of persons founded on grace (Fc. 20). This communion
of persons--in its larger sense as the universal Church, and in its smaller,
miniature sense as the domestic Church (family)--is a sacred call for union,
wherein each person through God's grace is connected with the Whole of
humanity with and through Jesus Christ (Fc. 21). So, just as the larger
communion of persons is sacramental, by virtue of God's Revelation, by virtue
that is of God's covenant of love with His people, so too each smaller
communion (each marriage, each family) is sacramental. The covenant
between the two spouses is a sacred sign of the Covenantal Love of God for
His people.

DOMESTIC CHURCH AS SACRAMENT: Rooted in Baptism

John Paul II explains that just as in Baptism a person is united with Christ through the Church and also united with the other members, similarly in Matrimony, a baptized man or woman "join in a familiar communion of persons in Christ." Thus, the marital union can be understood as a "specification of the broader communion of persons which is the Church." The matrimonial bond, therefore, can be described as "an intensification of the couple's Baptismal union with each other." These two communions are both rooted in the grace of the Holy Spirit and are essentially different aspects of the same reality.[1]

John Paul II is emphasizing that marriage and family are sacramental because they are constituted by a communion of giving which is sustained by grace in the same way that the greater communion (the People of God) is brought into being by the act of God's Revelation (Covenant) and his perfect Love (the Incarnation and Redemption).

Karl Rahner has explained that the grace of Covenant and the grace of conjugal love is one and the same. He describes that Christian marriage is "a real re-presentation of the unifying love of God for man in Christ." He states that: "In marriage the Church becomes present in the smallest community of redeemed mankind. Marriage creates the smallest true Church."[2]

DOMESTIC CHURCH AS SACRAMENT: In Its Totality

An important part of this understanding of marriage and family as sacrament is the fact that the relationship is **in essence** sacred. That is, it is **in its nature** a sacrament. It is not valid to define some one aspect of marriage as sacramental, such as to say that there is a spiritual dimension of the marriage, (i.e., to say that a spiritual dimension parallels a physical dimension and a psychological dimension). To do that fosters an invalid kind of dualism. Rather, what is being said here is that marriage and family life is by nature a sacrament, and that the various aspects of the relationship (i.e., the sexual, the psychological) are merely separate dimensions of the one over-all sacramental reality. The entirety of the marital relationship is sacred,--in all its sexual, physical, material, and psychological aspects.

All aspects of the relationship, then, are to be a sign (the indicative aspect of the two-fold nature of sacrament). However, all aspects of the relationship are also to be instrumental, in serving as vehicles of grace (the imperative aspect of sacrament). For, just as the universal Church on Earth is the Church militant, or the pilgrim Church, so too the domestic Church is "in process". That is to say, marriage and family life are a tremendous pilgrimage, an on-going journey which entails great effort and sacrifice, all aimed at greater unity and greater loving.

Thus, we see that the domestic Church is in process,--that it must be built! Just as the larger universal Church is being built up, is being renewed, and must be "ever new", so too the domestic church must be created and developed. Family life must be worked at, struggled with, and created anew at each phase of its development. All members, but with the parents certainly taking the lead, must dedicate themselves to building up the family.

DOMESTIC CHURCH: Its Mission

As domestic Church, the family has its special mission, by virtue of which it then shares in the threefold offices of Christ--priesthood, prophecy, and kingship. John Paul II explains that the proper activity or mission of every family is "to guard, reveal, and communicate love" (Fc. 17).

PRIESTLY MISSION

In light of this mission, the priestly office of the family can be said to consist of the giving of each member to the others. This begins with the marital couple, wherein each one must make a self-donation to his/her spouse. Each one must sacrifice his/her self in service to his/her spouse. Again, this effort of self-donation pertains to every facet of the marital relationship,--including their sexual activity, their material and financial matters, and their psychological relating, etc. Regarding the sexual self-giving John Paul II reminds us that the sexual act "is a lie when it is not the sign of and fruit of a total personal self-giving" (Fc. 11). It is, of course, the sexual self-giving which leads to procreation and the family. Within the family then, parents and children are called to make "sacrificial gifts of self" to each other. As they sacrifice themselves in service to each other-in giving birth, in feeding and maintaining life, in providing for material needs, in educating and in giving emotional support, etc.--the family practices its priesthood. Each member is a priest, in offering his/her true self, creations and endeavors, and self-giving to the other family members--and all to God. All the members are then offering themselves to each other and to God. Such self-giving, which must be merciful and entails limitless forgiving, is the essence of familial love. Clearly, since such a love is impossible due to man's fallen state, the family must be centered on Christ, since it is only through His grace that they will be able to faithfully sustain their communion with each other and grow in their relationships toward ever-greater love.[3]

PROPHETIC MISSION

The prophetic office of the domestic Church endows each family member with a responsibility to adhere to and give witness to the Gospel. That is, all the family members, led by the parents, must make a commitment to the message of Revelation. The most essential aspect of this for the family is for the parents to take responsibility for teaching the Gospel to their children, and educating them in the Faith. In this all-important task, parents must teach by instruction and by example. First of all, parents must impart to each child the fact that he/she is created in the image of God, that he/she thus has unique and inestimable worth and dignity, and that he/she is called into intimate relationship with God through Jesus Christ, and that each is called to know and to choose through truth and freedom. All of that constitutes what John Paul II describes as the family's task of helping each child to "discern his own vocation". Secondly, children must be educated as to love. They must be taught, by word and example, the Gospel message that active loving is "the fundamental and innate vocation of each human being," in the words of John Paul II (Fc. 11). Thus, parents must nurture and educate their children toward "the fullness of life" in light of the Gospel message.[4]

KINGLY MISSION

The kingly office of Christ, which consists of governance and leadership, applies to the domestic Church in two aspects. First of all, it entails the self-governance or self-directedness of each person such that each can live out an integrated and disciplined life, which is integrally connected with his/her capacity for self-giving to the other members. This, of course, relates to the leadership or shepherding role of the parents, in that they are called to guide each of their children to develop integration of self and self-discipline. This self-directedness and self-discipline--which together we might equate with healthy, authentic self-esteem--is an essential basis for the exercise of true freedom and mature decision-making. Again, it is the parents, in their marital relationship, who must provide example and direction in this area.

The second aspect of kingship involves governance or dominion over creation. This entails the acknowledgment that Earth and its resources if **for** human-kind, and that each person is entitled to share in Earth's riches. This calls for each family to provide for its own basic material needs by appropriately utilizing Earth's resources and by engaging in just and proper work. The primary responsibility, again, is on the parents, though appropriate coopera-tion between all family members in this regard is essential. In addition, the family is called to ensure that even as it uses its just share of material resources and goods, that all persons in the larger community have their rightful share of Earth's resources, such that all persons have the necessities for life by obtaining their rightful share of God's creation. Christ's kingship, in this regard, involves the "rehabilitation of the dignity of all people." Thus, as each family is called to the just and appropriate use of resources to meet its own needs, it is likewise called to work toward ensuring the same for the rest of the universal family of man.[5]

IMPLICATIONS OF THESE TEACHINGS

As described in the above summary, the Church is teaching us that Christian marriage and family life calls persons to an on-going life-long sacramental relationship which is inextricably bound up with God's grace and with the phenomena of Revelation to such an extent that it constitutes a true experience of Church. The family is the Church on its most fundamental level. It is insufficient, therefore, to define Christian marriage and family life according to characteristics which are solely human or secular.

A Christian marriage cannot be assessed solely according to the sexual behavior between the partners, for example, nor according to the emotional compatibility between the two--though both are certainly important aspects of the relationship. Rather, those two aspects, for example, must be taken merely as partial dimensions of a relational experience which by virtue of its sacramental quality transcends the merely human. The "marriage question", then, becomes not merely, "do I love this person enough?" (in the romantic sense), nor "are we psychologically compatible?", nor "will our lifestyle be sufficient or enjoyable?"---though all of those are certainly important questions which should definitely be part of the discernment about marriage. Those questions are essential, but not sufficient. The question of overall importance becomes "Do I will (do I choose) to commit myself to this relationship to such an extent that the relating becomes for me the primary communion through which I strive toward holiness?" Am I committed to this relationship to the degree that I am pledging a life-long effort toward the goal of having this relationship "show forth to all men Christ's living presence in the world"? Rather an awesome commitment, to put it mildly!

The understanding of Matrimony as an aspect of development of the Baptismal union, or as a specification and intensification of Baptism, suggests that prior to initiating the sacrament of Matrimony the Christian person needs to very seriously scrutinize his/her own life of Faith as a baptized believer. That is to say, should not each person considering Christian marriage first do an in-depth self-reflection as to his/her current degree of Faith commitment and his/her current level of holiness, prior to entering an "intensification" of Baptism? where am I on my Christian pilgrimage? Where am I as a member of Church? And am I at a point in my Faith life which is sufficient for Matrimony? Is my foundation (in Baptism) secure and developed to the point that I am now ready to move to a "new aspect of communion", to a "new dimension" of Church? Am I prepared for and disposed toward manifesting within my marital and family relationships a love which is a sacred symbol of the Covenantal Love of God for His people? Will my own journey toward greater holiness and that of my spouse be facilitated by our relationship? These are the deep questions of Faith which must be asked prior to Matrimony.

The pressures and demands on families in our contemporary Western society are indeed staggering. However, the Church is teaching us, as summarized above, that the Christian family cannot be defined by its solely human characteristics nor according to secular values. The family cannot be evaluated merely according to its physical, material, nor psychological dimensions. Rather, those various aspects can only be ascertained in light of its overall sacramental quality. The Christian family is called to create within itself (within its interpersonal relationships which are in essence sacrament) a full, though miniature-scale Church. This is indeed an incredible task! Yet we are told that it is possible, though solely through the help of God's grace. For it is only by virtue of God's grace, as manifested in all of Revelation, that the communion and love of family relationships is even possible. Thus, we might say that the primary task of the Christian family is to realize the fact of its essential sacramental nature, and to utilize its innate sacramental potential. One wonders if most Christian families are really aware of the fact that their inter-relationships are inherently sacred, and are sacrament, in both the indicative and imperative dimensions. On surmises that many Christian families fail to comprehend the fact that they **are** sacrament, and thus fail to utilize or develop the instruments of grace which they can be to each other. The challenge for the Christian family, then, seems to be for it to first come to a deeper awareness of its sacramental nature and then to operationalize that sacramentality within itself. John Paul II urges the Christian family to "become what you are" (Fc. 17). that exhortation seems pertinent, since it would appear that many of our Christian families today have failed to fully comprehend, and thus have failed to utilize, the awesome fact that **they** are sacrament, they **they** are Church.

ENDNOTES

1. Hogan, Richard M., & John M. LeVoir. *Covenant of Love; John Paul II on Sexuality, Marriage and the Family in the Modern World.* Garden City, New York: Image Books, 1986, p. 104.

2. Rahner, Karl. "Marriage as a Sacrament" in *Theology Digest,* Vol. 27; Spring 1969, p. 8.

3. Hogan & LeVoir, op. cit., pp. 105-107.

4. Hogan & LeVoir, op. cit., pp. 108-110.

5. Hogan & LeVoir, op. cit., pp. 110-112.

CHAPTER SIX

THE STRUCTURE AND EVOLUTION OF CALVIN'S DOCTRINE OF THE ATONEMENT:
Findings from Four Documents

Jonathan Tice
Western Theological Seminary

ABSTRACT

The structure and evolution of Calvin's approach to, and understanding of the atonement, explored, with special attention given to the òrigin of the *munus triplex*.

INTRODUCTION

In a previous paper ont he Holy Spirit in the Reformed Confessions I wrote, "If it is true that to study the work of the Holy Spirit in the Heidelberg Catechism is to study the comforter, and thus the whole document, this is even more the case in the Confession of 1967." It seems that key themes, at least in early reformation theological documents, pervade the structure of such writing as a whole. This being true oft he confessional literature, I have found that it is true of Calvin's understanding of the atonement as well. A thorough study of Calvin's doctrine of the atonement, especially in the *Institutes* (1559), is to study nothing less than the work of Christ!

To make matters worse, in a way, there is no shortage of literature on this subject. As a result, it would seem that no angle has been left uncovered. At one important point in my intellectual development a kind professor said to m e something like this: "When wading through scholarly opinion becomes an overwhelming and minimally productive task, go back to the text and work with it, reading it carefully and posing it thoughtful questions. Chances are you will learn more."[1] That is what I have attempted to do here, in looking afresh at how Calvin describes the atonement. I have used the *Institutes* of 1536, the Catechism of 1538, the Geneva Catechism of 1541, and the final,

1559 edition of the *Institutes*. In each of these documents the atonement is addressed within the context of the Apostles Creed. I have focused on those passages as they provide a means of comparison. It became clear as I worked with the different texts that Calvin's approach to the atonement had changed over the years. The material was worked over in different ways and one gets a different feel from each document.

Robert Peterson's book, *Calvin's Doctrine of the Atonement*, goes into great depth in describing the various themes that Calvin uses to describe this important work of Christ. He structured his work around the office of Christ, emphasizing six biblical themes that Calvin uses to explain the atonement. Of the office of Christ he writes:

> The concept of "office" to describe Christ's saving activity has a long history. In the patristic period both the twofold office (Christ as king and priest) and the threefold office (Christ as prophet, king, and priest) are found. Calvin's writings show a movement from the use of the *munus duplex* (twofold office) to that of the *munus triplex*. He used the twofold office idea in the first (1536) edition of the *Institutes* In his treatise "Instruction in the Faith" of 1537, the twofold office appeared again. In the 1539 Institutes the prophetic office occurred for the first time, but it was not yet directly related to the title "Christ." In the 1545 Institutes, the Catechism of 1543, and the final (1559) edition of the *Institutes*, the threefold office appeared as Calvin's exposition of the messianic name.[2]

Although elements of these six themes can be found in the documents I studied, I maintain that Calvin's thought is not so easily structured and would suggest that these titles are products of a projection of systematic theology back onto Calvin. In a significant way, the thematic appropriation of Calvin's writings obscures the dynamic detail of the reformer's thought. This is a useful historical summary of a key element in Calvin's theology, and Peterson adds six further themes to it: (1) Christ the obedient second Adam, (2) Christ the victor, (3) Christ our legal substitute, (4) Christ our sacrifice, (5) Christ our merit, (6) Christ our example. Most notably, as will be seen, the Christus Victor theme is more appropriate in discussing Aulén's work on the subject than in isolating a "topic" in Calvin. In essence, Calvin is not working with an order or template of dogma. He is exegeting and animating the latent material in the creed, in which he finds the sum of Christian belief.

It may be contended that I am splitting a hair in thus maintaining that confessional theology and systematic theology have different nuances to their structure. Yet I think that if William J. Bouwsma's critique is to be taken seriously, that is, that the twentieth century reader may be too ready to find a system at work in Calvin and therefore loose the sense of dynamic tension that is evident in the text,[3] then perhaps we should investigate Calvin's actual approach to the creed rather than try to indicate how it fits into categories we expect to find. That is what I have tried to do here, to look carefully at what Calvin finds in the creed.

CALVIN'S EARLY APPROACH TO THE ATONEMENT

THE ATONEMENT IN THE *INSTITUTES* OF 1536:   An Approach Via Christ's Nature

Calvin's early discussion of the atonement in the 1536 *Institutes* takes place in the context of his discussion of the creed. What is more important, it occurs within the overarching context of Christian faith. It is particularly important to note that Calvin uses the first article oft he creed to discuss the providence of God, more specifically the will of God toward the faithful. He writes: "By faith are we to be persuaded that whatever happens to us, happy or sad, prosperous or adverse, whether it pertains tot he body or to the soul, comes to us from him (sin only excepted which is to be imputed to our own wickedness); also by his protection we are kept safe, defended, and preserved from any unfriendly force causing us harm."[4]   That notion of persuasion comes up again when Calvin asserts that the creed itself is a document by which we can be taught the true faith with "utter certainty." In the last sentence of the section Calvin writes: "Therefore, whatever may finally happen, we are never to doubt or lose faith that we have in him a propitious and benevolent Father, and no lesser to await salvation from him. For it is something utterly certain and true that the faith we are each of us taught to hold by this first part of the Creed is the right faith."[5]   Thus, for Calvin there are two parts to knowing, or being persuaded: through the orthodox teachings of the church and by God. In a certain sense, for Calvin, as for other reformers such as Bullinger, in scripture viewed as the word of God, or in a document such as the creed that directly reflects that word, God is also there, making it possible by the working of the Holy Spirit to appropriate and be persuaded through human language.

Having asserted both the orthodoxy of the creed and the certainty of faith in God's will, Calvin is free to move on to the foundation of the atonement, still in the *Institutes of 1536*. In this edition of the *Institutes* Calvin's overarching concern is the incarnation, that is, a correct understanding of how Christ was fully God and fully human. Peterson aptly observes the importance of this foundation for the correct understanding of the atonement when he writes: "In the thought of John Calvin there is an essential precondition for the atonement; without it no atonement could have been accomplished. It is likewise that which makes the atonement intelligible—it gives Christ's work its meaning and force. That prerequisite for atonement in Calvin is the incarnation: *God became a man for our salvation*. When we understand the meaning and ramifications of that statement, we will be ready to examine the atonement itself."[6]   David Willis phrases this point in somewhat more extensive language when he writes: "The *extra-calvinisticum* emphasizes that the God at work in Jesus Christ is one and the same with the God who sustains and orders the universe....Calvin is asserting that Christ is able to be God for us because he does not cease to be God over us in the Incarnation and because the humanity of Christ never ceases to be our humanity in the movement of God towards us."[7]   Or, as Calvin put it: "The Word was therefore made flesh [John 1:14]; he who was God likewise became man so that the very same one might be both man and God, not by confusion of substance, but by unity of person."[8]

Perhaps the most important phrase in the above understandings of Calvin's view of the atonement is his own: "not by confusion of substance, but by unity of person." As Bouwsma points out, confusion is a key theme for Calvin. For the atonement to be efficacious, the incarnation as the foundation for it must be one in which there is no confusion of substance. One could read this as a type of neo-Platonism, as if the earthly realm of the body and the ethereal realm, the realm of forms, can never mingle. Yet, Calvin was forced by his orthodoxy to move beyond that view of reality, a view which had earlier lead to Gnostism. Nevertheless, even within his orthodoxy there remains a tension. Bouwsma offers an explanation when he writes this of Calvin:

> The notion that what ails the world is confusion had much practical value for Calvin. Confusion, unlike sin, can be remedied, at least symbolically, by various ordering devices at human disposal. Thus, when Calvin associated disorder with obscurity, he could conceive of correcting it by sharpening the contours of the various entities composing the world; once one thing has been clearly distinguished, physically or conceptually, from the others, it can be assigned its proper place in the order of things. Descartes was not the first European, or even the first Frenchman, who craved clear

and distinct ideas. Calvin's concern about such matters is
one source of his famous clarity of style; he stabilized the
meanings of words, as Higman has pointed out, but therefore also the structures of the universe he inhabited, by such
linguistic devices as frugality in the use of adjectives.[9]

Clearly then, in the *Institutes of 1536* Calvin is quite concerned with Christology as a foundation for a proper understanding of the atonement; he there
devotes a lengthy discussion to the topic even within his discussion of the
creed. In the 1559 edition of the *Institutes* he deals with the incarnation
separately and has it precede discussion of the creed. My investigation of
Calvin's discussion of the atonement in the creed began with the *Catechism
of 1538*. Thus, when I went back to the *Institutes of 1536*, I was struck to find
significant portions of Calvin's basic thought that were absent in the later
work.

Two things stand out in this regard. The first point has to do with the Trinity.
The question of persona and hypostasis in the Trinitarian controversies is
similar to that of the Christological controversies in that the discussion centers
on a correct description of the essential Trinity. I find it strikingly consistent,
given Calvin's concern over "confusion of substance," that a description of the
Trinity appears prominently in his 1536 work. Moreover, it stands out within
the context of the first article of the creed. Calvin writes: "Moreover, the
Father is particularly called Creator of heaven and earth [Heb. 1:2, 10]
because (as we previously said) of the distinction of properties, whereby the
beginning of acting is referred to the Father that he may be said indeed to act
by himself, but through the Word and his Wisdom, yet in his Power. That
nevertheless there was a common action of the three persons in creating the
world is made plain by that statement of the Father: "Let us make man in our
image and likeness" [Gen. 1:26]. In these words he is not taking counsel with
the angels, not speaking with himself, but addressing his Wisdom and
Power."[10]

The second point that stands out has to do with this understanding of Jesus
as the only son. In the section devoted to this idea Calvin gives sharper
distinction to his recurring theme of believers as children of God adopted by
grace. The distinction here also turns on a proper understanding of the
nature of Christ, that is, a correct understanding and appropriation of the
incarnation. Accordingly Calvin writes: "By this we confess that we believe
in Jesus Christ who we are convinced is the only Son of God the Father. He
is the Son, not as believers are by adoption and grace only—but by nature,
begotten of the Father from eternity. When we call him 'only' Son we are

stinguishing him from all others. In as much as he is God, he is one God with the Father, of the same nature and substance or essence, not otherwise than, distinct as to the person which he has as his very own, distinct from the Father [Ps. 100:3a]."[11]

A striking result of Calvin's approach to the atonement by way of the incarnation is a minimization of descriptive material on the *actions* of Christ in relation to the atonement (especially when compared with the *Catechism of 1538*—see charts below). What emerges instead, is a propositional style due largely to Calvin's abhorrence of confusion of natures. That is, the nature of Christ is set up over and against human nature as being able to accomplish the redemption of humanity. Thus he moves from the proposition, "who could," to an answer based on the nature of Christ.[12]

Who could... Swallow up death	**But...**Life itself
Who could... Conquer sin	**But...**Righteousness itself

Calvin goes on to assert: "Who is life or righteousness but God alone? Therefore our most merciful Lord, when he willed that we be redeemed, made himself our Redeemer."[13] This theme of becoming the atonement continues when he writes: "...man, who by his disobedience had become lost, should by obedience remove his confusion, satisfy God's justice, and pay the penalties of sin. Accordingly our Lord came forth, true man. He took on the person of Adam, received his name in order to show himself obedient to the Father on man's behalf, to set our flesh as satisfaction for God's Justice, to pay the penalty of sin."[14]

THE ATONEMENT IN THE *CATECHISM* OF 1538: An Approach Via Christ's Actions, or "The Great Exchange"

If Calvin's treatment of the atonement in 1536 can be characterized as expressing concern regarding the nature of Christ and the related question of who Christ is for us, the Catechism of 1538 can be characterized as Calvin's working out the question of what Christ does for us. Throughout the treatment he takes care to specify how Christ's actions accomplish something for us. Most often Christ's action is depicted as the taking on of something on our behalf, in which we would be unsuccessful, and succeeding for us. As an example, he indicates that Christ died that he might conquer death for us.

It is particularly interesting that Calvin here gives a brief explanation of the atonement within his discussion of the phrase, *Born of the virgin Mary*. He articulates the *munus duplex* and adds the results of Jesus' incarnation. Here again we see Calvin articulating the practical aspects of abstract doctrine. The incarnation is thus made a real and living belief for people here and now in contrast to an event merely of the past. this is important, for Calvin wants to avoid a mere forensic doctrine of the atonement. For Calvin theology, like faith, is an animated, living thing, not merely a set of propositions.

INCARNATION:

Christ...	Result on Human Beings
Is made King	To protect us
Is made Priest	To reconcile us to the Father
Flesh put in order	To make us sons [and daughters] of God
Received our poverty	To transfer his wealth to us
Submitted to our weakness	To strengthen us by his Power[15]
Accepted our mortality	To give us immortality
Descended to earth	To raise us to heaven
Man in Sin	Christ like us in all things yet without sin

The incarnation is as important here as it is in the *Institutes of 1536*, yet it is given in short hand, almost as if Calvin were saying "Cf. my exhaustive treatment of this in the earlier work." Christ is described as true son of Abraham, true son of David, true man and is claimed to be the one promised by the law and prophets.

The table below illustrates the movement Calvin accentuates between Christ's actions and our benefits. In explaining *Suffered under Pontius Pilate, was crucified, dead, and buried; he descended into hell*, each action of Christ is shown to have an effect on humanity. The formula "that he might" occurs repeatedly in this section, serving as a refrain which lifts Christ's actions out of the past and shows their effect on us today.

Christ is or does:	That he might _____ for us
By being obedient	He wipes out the effect of our disobedience.
By offering himself as a Sacrifice	1. In order that God's wrath and Justice might be appeased by his death for all times. 2. In order that believers might be eternally sanctified and God's eternal satisfaction fulfilled.[16]
Poured out his sacred blood	1. In payment for our redemption. 2. In order that God's anger might be extinguished. 3. In order that our iniquity might be cleansed.
Judged	That by his condemnation we might be absolved from judgment.
Crucified	That he might bear our curse.
Died	That he might conquer death for us.
Swallowed death	So death could not swallow us.
Buried	That he might bury us from sin.
Descended into hell	That he might feel the dread of Divine punishment for us.[17]
Intercedes with God's wrath	1. That he might satisfy God's justice. 2. That he might pay our debts and lift our penalties

In all, the tables above illustrate twenty-two effects of the work of Christ for us. Clearly Calvin perceived a deep richness in both the work of Christ and in the summary witness to it the creed. It is impossible to imagine that Calvin recited the creed with the simple understanding and ho hum appearance that one sees so often in churches today. Rather for Calvin the creed was rich with meaning, providing a mere outline of the great work that Christ took on for us.

THE ATONEMENT IN THE *GENEVA CATECHISM* (1541): The Title of Christ

If the richness of the creed is implied by Calvin's exegesis of it in the *Catechism* of 1538, it is made explicit in the Geneva Catechism. The question and answer numbered 15 indicate that the sum of all knowledge of God can be found in the creed. It is interesting that in question #55 Calvin offers an explanation for the omission of the life of Christ in the creed. He writes:

> 55. *M.   Why do you go immediately from His birth to His death, passing over the whole history of his life?*
>
> *C.* Because nothing is said here about what belongs properly to the substance of his redemption.

It is clear from this passage that for Calvin the substance of the knowledge of God is the sum of the redemptive action of Christ, that is, Christology proper. Here Calvin's practicality shows through. The child is asked to explain the importance of each part of the creed, and thus as part of the description of the title "Christ" the *munus triplex* is clearly stated.[18]

> 34. *M.   What, next, is meant by the name Christ?*
>
> *C.* By the title His office is still better expressed—for it signifies that He was anointed by the Father to be ordained King, Priest, and Prophet.

It is interesting that here Calvin does not continue to speak of Christ as King directly but changes to a discussion of the kingdom itself. His discussion of the Priesthood and the Prophetic office is split into two parts, the first part having to do with the title itself; the second having to do with the benefits we derive from it. The sequence, then, is as follows:

Q 37	The Kingdom
Q 38	The priesthood
Q 39	Christ the Prophet
Q 40 + 41	The benefits to humans of these offices
Q 42	The benefits of the Kingdom
Q 43	The Benefits of His Priesthood
Q 44	The benefits of His prophetic office

He then concludes:

45. M. You would conclude, then, that the title of Christ includes three offices which God has given to His Son, in order to communicate virtue and fruit to his faithful people?

C. That is so.

This is clearly a full *munus triplex*, and it is important because of its clarity, elegance and order. We do not have here the type of abstraction that is encountered in the *Institutes of 1536*, nor is there a didactic structure as was found in the Catechism of 1538.[19] There is also an evolution regarding the context of the atonement. Just as Calvin now treats the creed in the context of faith and the knowledge of God, he has moved the atonement proper to place it under the discussion of the forgiveness of sin and the doctrine of the church. The key questions in this regard are numbers 102-104.

102. M. What do you understand by this word "forgiveness"?
C. That God by His pure goodness forgives and pardons the sins of believers, so that they are not brought to account before His judgment, in order to be punished.

103. M. Hence it follows that it is not at all through our own satisfaction that we desire to have God's pardon?
C. That is true; for the Lord Jesus has made payment and born the punishment. We on our part could not make any recompense to God, but may only receive pardon for all our misdeeds through the pure generosity of God.

104. M. Why do you insert this article after the Church?
C. Because no man obtains pardon for his sins without being previously incorporated into the people of God.

Jansen's contribution to the discussion of the *munus triplex*.

In his book *Calvin's Doctrine of the Work of Christ,* Jansen provides a through discussion of the *munus triplex* in Calvin's thought. In that work he pulls together observations on the *munus triplex* from a number of scholars and theologians. I have found Jansen to be helpful in confirming my own observations about the *munus triplex* in Calvin's thought and in broadening my understanding of the way Calvin approached different aspects of theology. Jansen begins his discussion with the important observation that for Calvin the work of Christ is *one work.* That is to say, the *munus triplex* should not be taken to indicate that the work of Christ is fragmented into three works, each under its own heading. He further points out that it would be a mistake to read into the *munus triplex* a Trinitarian (and I would add a potentially modal) progression. In this regard he writes:

> John Henry Newman suggested: "It will be observed, moreover, that in these offices He also represents to us the Holy Trinity: for in His proper character He is the priest, and so to His Kingdom He has it from the Father, and as to His prophetical office, He exercises it by the Spirit. The Father is the King, the Son the Priest, and the Holy Ghost the Prophet." [from Newman, "The Three Offices of Christ," in *The Worlds' Great Sermons*] It is fair to say, however, that the doctrine of the three offices was not intended for such speculative use but rather was meant only to express in coherent fashion the unitary work of Christ as the Redeemer. Great care was taken to insist that Christ fulfills these offices not successively (though their order may appear in greater successive clarity during His life) but rather simultaneously. Because Christ is one, He is not now a prophet, now a priest, or now a king; rather, He is always at every moment prophet, priest, and king.[20]

Moreover, Jansen argues that the work of Christ is a representative action. He states: "Jesus came not to do His own will; He came as the Lord's Anointed who was divinely commissioned with a redemptive task."[21]   In further support of this point he quotes Emil Brunner: "Christ is known in what he *does.* 'Revelation, Atonement, and Lordship are the three aspects of one and the same reality, of what God in Jesus Christ has done, and will do for us.'[22] Peterson takes this view a step further, and quotes Karl Barth when he writes:

The offices of Christ "are not three compartments." While maintaining the distinctions between the three, "it is necessary to see their connection, each one always implies the two others." [Karl Barth, *La Confession de foi de l'églis, p. 35.*] Thus Christ's work of reconciliation must be seen as the basis for His prophetic proclamation and the royal gifts of eternal life and protection He bestows on His church. Christ as prophet functions as inner teacher to actualize the priestly work of reconciliation and thereby usher sinners into the kingdom of God. Christ he king protects those who were purchased by Christ the priest and called by Christ the prophet. It is in terms of kingship that the eschatological consummation of the other two offices will occur. Those whom Christ reconciled to God and for whom He presently intercedes will experience consummate peace with God in His very presence. Those whom Christ as inner teacher has enlightened to receive the gospel will enjoy the eternal fruits of that Good News in the eschatological kingdom of God.[23]

One begins to wonder why Calvin would use a threefold exposition of the messianic name when, so many theologians regard it as descriptive of one work and not three. Jansen provides something of an answer to this question when he says: "Nevertheless, it is possible to trace a fairly definite doctrine of Christ's work in terms of what was seen in the messianic name. It is in this way that we can see the antecedents of Calvin's doctrine. Expositions of the messianic name do not necessarily mean definitive categories for dogmatics, but they do indicate what is regarded as essential to the work of redemption. In a sense, therefore, a history of the doctrine of the offices of Christ will be a history of the exegesis of the messianic title."[24] This is a very important point and serves as a critique of later Calvinism's attempts to find rigid categories when, in all probability, Calvin was describing the implicit elements of a given theme.[25] Jansen offers an explanation as to why Calvin might have developed this threefold description of the messianic title. He recalls: "Calvin is anxious to find an adequate biblical foundation for the church's ministry that will preserve the principle of the priesthood of all believers while yet safeguarding the ministerial order against a Roman denial of its authenticity and an Anabaptist repudiation of church orders."[26] If Jansen is correct in this regard, then here we find Calvin, as he does so often, taking a middle position between two extremes. Jansen states:

In itself it does not prove anything that Calvin should have devoted only one short chapter to the three offices in his last

edition of the *Institutes,* and then should make no further
reference to the formula. After all, he usually speaks of the
mediatorial office in the singular since the work of Christ is
a unitary work. *"Officium Christi est, rect nos ad patrem
manu ducere."* ["De Scandalis quibus hodie plerique abster-
rentur nonnulli etiam alienantur a pura evangelii doctrina,"
in *C.O.* 8, p. 10] Christ has but one purpose in his coming—to bring us to God. Accordingly, it is not surprising that
Calvin should follow the chapter on the three offices with a
longer chapter entitled, "Christ's execution of the office of a
Redeemer to procure our salvation." Calvin would never
have had patience with the over-refinements of some of his
followers who sought so to analyze the various offices that
the work of Christ becomes "departmentalized"—and deper-
sonalized.[27]

He goes on: "To sum up: In spite of the fact that Calvin suggests the formula
of the three offices in the later editions of his *Institutes* and *Catechism,* he
does not himself make any real use of the formula."[28]

In conclusion, Calvin clearly does use the *munus triplex,* and thus some
rationale should be available which at least describes its potential meaning for
Calvin. Jansen proposes that the key to the threefold office is not so much
in the titles themselves as in Calvin's understanding of office itself. Accordingly he writes:

To understand such phrases, however, two things need to be
remembered. First of all, we must recall Calvin's free us of
the word "office." [So, for example, Calvin will speak of
God as "undertaking the office of a teacher." Comm. John
vi. 45.] In the second place, we must remember Calvin's
understanding of the place and purpose of prophecy. The
prophets of the Old Testament are the interpreters of the
law. "So it is seen that the office of the prophets was not
only to predict things to come, but also to give good instruction to the people, to exhort them to repentance, and to
edify them in faith, so we see that he prophets not only said,
'this thing is going to happen.' But they ratified the covenant
of God by which He had adopted the people of Israel, they
announced the coming of the Redeemer on whom rested the
expectation of all the children of God. And then they
comforted the afflicted, telling them of the promises of

God's grace, yet also they warned the people when the people disobeyed, they made known their faults and transgressions, they called sinners to the judgment of God to humble them. All these things constituted the office of prophets." [Fifth Sermon on Deut. xviii., *C.O.* 27, p. 529][29]

Moreover, Jansen adds:

There is a deeper reason. For Calvin the Word of God is always a redemptive word. True knowledge of God always means commitment to God. Since redemption is a kingly and priestly work, its ministration through teaching must also have this double character. It is thus a *kingly* function. "Thus the gift of prophecy in Saul was a kind of mark of royalty; so that he might not ascend the throne without credentials." [Comm. Num. xi,. 24. The reference is to I Sam. x. 0. For the same emphasis, cf. homily on I Sam. ii. 10, *C.O.* 29, p. 314] It is also a *priestly* function, for "there is no priesthood without doctrine of teaching, and no priest except he who faithfully performs his office as a teacher." [Comm. Mal. ii. 9] "These two things are, as they say, inseparable—the office of the priesthood and teaching...we hence see that all this belongs peculiarly to the sacerdotal office." [Comm. Mal. ii. 6][30]

Thus, Calvin's use of the threefold office primarily provides a descriptive structure. Calvin uses this structure to appropriate the theological significance of scripture. His theology then, goes on to describe the unity of the work of Christ.

CALVIN'S FINAL NUANCES ON THE OFFICE OF CHRIST: The Atonement in the *Institutes of 1559*

In the *Institutes of 1559* the office of Christ has been expanded a great deal from what Calvin indicated in the earlier writings I examined. Here I simply include points that stand out as quite unique in comparison to Calvin's earlier treatment of the name of Christ.

Calvin shows here a full *munus triplex,* but he does more than that. For Calvin doctrine had to have a "purpose and use." That is, there is a practical implication in these statements for us here and now. These statements are

not a matter simply of correct historical understanding; they have benefit for
our lives today.   Thus Calvin continually and consistently moves between
abstract and concrete, between the office of Christ and the benefits of that
office for us.   In doing so he connects Christology with a number of other
doctrines, making it almost impossible to remain in only one section of the
Institutes at a time.   In this sense Calvin's discourse is much like that of
Scripture, wherein one thing inevitably leads to another.   Accordingly, Calvin
writes of the office of Christ: "There fore, in order that faith may find a firm
basis for salvation in Christ, and thus rest in him, this principle must be laid
down: the office enjoined upon Christ by the Father consists of three parts.
For he was given to be prophet, king, and priest.   Yet it would be of little
value to know these names without understanding their purpose and use."[31]

It is interesting that the foundation of the threefold office as Calvin expounded
here is attached to the anointing of Jesus with oil. He explains: "Now it is to
be noted that the title "Christ" pertains to these three offices: for we know
that under the law prophets as well as priests and kings were anointed with
holy oil."[32]   In a parallel passage in the Catechism of 1538 he had written:
"He was endowed with all the graces of the Holy Spirit, which are marked int
he Scriptures with the name 'oil' for the reason that without them we waste
away, dry and barren."[33]   In the *Institutes* he continues with this theme by
describing its implications for the church.   "We see that he was anointed by
the Spirit to be herald and witness of the Father's grace.   And not that in the
common way—for he is distinguished from other teachers with a similar office.
On the other hand, we must note this: he received anointing, not only for
himself that he might carry out the office of teaching, but for his whole body
that the power of the Spirit might be present in the continuing preaching of
the gospel."[34]   Here Calvin is connecting the work of Christ with the work of
the Spirit, especially in relation to the preaching of the Gospel, and thus
faith, as well as the way that the providence of God works to protect the
faithful, that is the church.   He states: "Therefore, whenever we hear of
Christ as armed with eternal power, let us remember that the perpetuity of
the church is secure in this protection. Hence, amid the violent agitation with
which it is continually troubles, amid the grievous and frightful storms that
threaten it with unnumbered calamities, it still remains safe."[35]

Thus we can see, as far as this paper has treated the matter, that for Calvin
the work of Christ, which is an expression of the providence of God for the
faithful here and now, ultimately resides in the church, for whom the work
was done. For Calvin the work of Christ then, is the work of Christ by the
power of the Spirit beneficial for us now. The atonement for Calvin is never
a mere description of a past action; rather, by his whole approach to the topic

we can plainly see that it is viewed as an integral part of our life of faith, an action then which God, out of a free gift of love, has made efficacious for us today. It is true that Calvin insists at one point: "For this reason we ought to know that the happiness promised us in Christ does not consist in outward advantages—such as leading a joyous and peaceful life, having rich possessions, being safe from all harm, and abounding with delights such as the flesh commonly longs after. No, our happiness belongs to the heavenly life![36] Yet Calvin does not stop with an other-worldly heavenly life only; he goes on implicitly to charge his readers to pursue actively spirituality, that is, to live the Christian life. "In the world the prosperity and well-being of a people depend partly on an abundance of all good things, and domestic peace, partly on strong defenses that protect them from outside attacks. In like manner, Christ enriches his people with all things necessary for the eternal salvation of should and fortifies them with courage to stand unconquerable against all the assaults of spiritual enemies. Form this we infer that he rules-inwardly and outwardly-more for our own sake than his. Hence we are furnished, as far as God knows to be expedient for us, with the gifts of the Spirit, which we lack by nature. By these first fruits we may perceive that we are truly joined to God in perfect blessedness. Then, relying upon the power of the same Spirit, let us not doubt that we shall always be victorious over the devil, the world, and every kind of harmful thing."[37]

ENDNOTES

1. I believe I can reasonably attribute this to J. Christian Beker, professor of New Testament at Princeton Theological Seminary.

2. Peterson, p. 27.

3. William J. Bouwsma, *John Calvin: A Sixteenth Century Thinker.* pp. 5ff.

4. *Institutes 1536 Ed.,* Battles, p. 49.

5. *Institutes 1536 Ed.,* Battles, p. 49.

6. Peterson, p. 11.

7. Willis, pp. 6f, quoted in Peterson p. 14.

8. *Institutes 1536 Ed.,* Battles, p. 52.

9. Bouwsma, p. 34.

10. Battles, p. 50.

11. Battles, p. 50.

12. *Institutes 1536 Ed.,* Battles, p. 51.

13. *Institutes 1536 Ed.,* Battles, p. 51.

14. *Institutes 1536 E.,* Battles, p. 51.

15. "Power" is an implicit shorthand expression for the work of the Holy Spirit.

16. It is important to note that for Calvin the sacrificial aspect of the atonement incorporates *both* Justification and Sanctification. There is no split here; on the contrary, the two doctrines are held tightly together. Thus he can discuss sanctification as related directly to the saving, justifying act of Christ's atonement.

17. It is important to note here however that Calvin *always,* that is to say in every document I have read, goes out of his way to make clear that "God was never angry with the Son...."

18. Apparently Peterson did not fine this point to be of importance, as the first occurrence he lists of the *munus triplex* is the Catechism of 1543, two years after the *Geneva Catechism!* Cf. Peterson, p. 27.

19. The *Geneva Catechism* (1541 has apparently been overlooked by scholars in their search for the origins of the *munus triplex.* Jansen traces the history of the doctrine, omitting the *Geneva Catechism,* and finds the earliest threefold exposition of the divine name in 1543; he writes: "In the edition of 1539, however, the prophetic office of Christ begins to appear, though it is not yet explicitly added to the other two [*C.O.* 1, pp. 513, 515]. This passage represents an interesting transition in Calvin's doctrine. The three offices of prophet, priest, and king are suggested as forming our heritage by grace. The prophetic office, however, is not yet directly related to the messianic name.... The change is also reflected in the Catechism of 1543 (French edition) and 1545 (Latin edition), as the messianic title is now explained: 'By this title is clearly declared His office. He was anointed by the heavenly Father to be

ordained as King, Priest or Sacrifice, and Prophet.' [*C.O.* 6, p. 19]," Jansen, pp. 41-42.

20. Jansen, p. 17.

21. Jansen p. 19. In a footnote to this point Jansen adds "Even Schleiermacher insists: 'But these expressions are not to be put on one level with other pictorial expressions, manifestly their purpose is to be sought in the comparison they indicate between the achievements of Christ in the corporate life founded by Him and those by which the Jewish people of the theocracy was represented and held together, and this comparison is not even to-day to be neglected in the system of doctrine.' *The Christian Faith.*, second editions of 1830, trans. H. R. Macintosh and J. S. Stewart (Edinburgh, T & T Clark, 1928), p. 439."

22. Jansen, p. 22. Quoting Emil Brunner, *The Christian Doctrine of Creation and Redemption* Westminster Press, 1952, p. 305.

23. Peterson, p. 38.

24. Jansen, p. 25.

25. Jansen supports this observation when he notes: "I believe later Calvinism has too easily confined Calvin's doctrine of atonement to Anselmic terms. No language, indeed, can fully represent the consequences and efficacy of Christ's death." Jansen, p. 90.

26. Jansen, pp. 45046.

27. Jansen, p. 52.

28. Jansen, p. 59.

29. Jansen, p. 98.

30. Jansen, p. 99.

31. *Institutes* II.15.1, p. 494.

32. *Institutes* II.15.2, p. 495.

33. Catechism of 1538, #20.ii.

34. *Institutes* II.15.2, p. 496. One has to wonder what the implications of Calvin's emphasis on anointing with the Holy Spirit are for the continuing dialogue between mainline and Pentecostal groups.

35. *Institutes* II.15.3, p. 497.

36. *Institutes* II.15.4, p. 498.

37. *Institutes* II.15.4, p. 498.

BIBLIOGRAPHY

Battles, Ford Lewis, and I. John Hesselink. *An Introduction to Calvin's Theology: Based primarily on Ford Lewis Battles' translation of Calvin's first Catechism (1538).* Unpublished manuscript, third edition. Western Theological Seminary, 19990.

Bouwsma, William J. *John Calvin: A Sixteenth Century Portrait.* New York: Oxford University Press, 1988.

Calvin, John. *Institution of the Christian Religion 1536.* Translated and edited by Ford Lewis Battles. Grand Rapids: Eerdmans, 1986.

_____. *Institutes of the Christian Religion.* Edited by John T. McNeill, translated by Ford Lewis Battles, 2 vol. Library of Christian Classics vol. 20-21. Philadelphia: Westminster Press, 1960.

Jansen, John F. *Calvin's Doctrine of the Work of Christ.* London: J. Clarke, 1956.

McKee, Anne E., and Brian G. Armstrong eds. *Probing the Reformed Tradition: Historical Studies in Honor of Edward A. Dowey, Jr.* Louisville: Westminster/John Knox. 1989.

Peterson, Robert A. *Calvin's Doctrine of the Atonement.* Phillipsburg: Presbyterian and Reformed Publishing Co., 1983.

Torrance, Thomas T. *The School of Faith: The Catechisms of the Reformed Church.* London: James Clarke and Co., 1959.

Wendel, François. *Calvin: Origins and Development of His Religious Thought.*
Durham: Labyrinth Press, 1987.

DATE DUE

			Printed in USA